Christmas
at the
Nativity

Christmas
at the
Nativity

Pope Francis

NEW CITY PRESS

Published in the United States by New City Press
202 Comforter Blvd., Hyde Park, NY 12530
© 2023 New City Press (English translation)

Translated from the original Italian edition
Il Mio Presepe: Vi racconto i personaggi del Natale

© 2023 Dicastero per la Comunicazione–Libreria Editrice Vaticana

© 2023 Mondadori Libri S.p.A., Milano

Vatican translations used with permission.

Cover design and layout by Miguel Tejerina – Gary Brandl

Library of Congress Control Number: 2023943973

ISBN: 978-1-56548-576-1 (Paperback)
ISBN: 978-1-56548-577-8 (E-book)

4th Printing, September 2024

Printed in the United States of America

Contents

Introduction 7

The Nativity Scene............................ 11

The Child Jesus................................. 18

Mary 40

Joseph...................................... 52

Bethlehem 59

The Stable....................................62

The Angels....................................67

The Shepherds.................................68

The Light..................................... 74

The Magi 79

The Star 93

Herod 98

The Holy Family................................ 104

The Various Statues............................ 113

The Christmas Tree 115

Christmas......................... 117

Epilogue 133

Sources 135

Introduction

Twice I have gone to visit Greccio.

The first time I went to learn about the place where St. Francis of Assisi invented the Nativity scene, something that also marked my childhood: in my parents' house in Buenos Aires, this sign of Christmas always was put up, even before the tree.

The second time I gladly returned to that place, in the province of Rieti, to sign the apostolic letter *Admirabile signum,* on the meaning and significance of the Nativity scene today.

On both occasions I felt a special emotion emanating from the grotto, where a medieval fresco can be admired, one side of it depicting the night of Bethlehem, and the other depicting the night of Greccio.[1]

The excitement of that sight prompts me to delve deeper into the Christian mystery that loves to hide within what is infinitely small.

Indeed, the Incarnation of Jesus Christ remains the heart of God's revelation, although it is easily forgotten that its unfolding is so unobtrusive to the point of going unnoticed.

Littleness, in fact, is the way to encounter God.

On the tombstone of St. Ignatius of Loyola it is written, *Non coerceri a maximo, sed contineri a minimo, divinum est* (Not to be limited by the greatest, and yet to be contained in the tiniest—this is the divine). In short, one should not be frightened of the big things; one should go forward and take into account the smaller things.

---

1. In 1223, when St. Francis created the first Nativity scene (see also p. 14). -Ed.

This is why safeguarding the spirit of the Nativity scene becomes a healthy immersion in the presence of God manifested in the small, sometimes trivial and repetitive, everyday things. Knowing how, in order to understand and choose God's ways, to renounce what seduces but leads down a bad path is the task we face. In this regard, discernment is a great gift, and we must never tire of asking for it in prayer. The shepherds in the manger are those who welcome God's surprise and live in wonder at their encounter with him, adoring him: in littleness they recognize the face of God. Humanly we are all inclined to seek greatness, but it is a gift to know how to really find it: to know how to find greatness in that smallness that God so loves.

In January 2016 I met the youth of Rieti at the very haven of the Infant Jesus, just above the Nativity shrine. I reminded them, and everyone today, that on Christmas night there are two signs that guide us in recognizing Jesus. One is the sky full of stars. There are many of those stars, an infinite number, but among them all a special star stands out, the one that prompted the Magi to leave their homes and begin a journey, a journey that would lead them where they did not know. It happens the same way in our lives: at a certain moment some special "star" invites us to make a decision, to make a choice, to begin a journey. We must forcefully ask God to show us that star that draws us toward something more than our habits, because that star will lead us to contemplate Jesus, that child who is born in Bethlehem and who wants our full happiness.

On that night, made holy by the Savior's birth, we find another powerful sign: the smallness of God. The angels point out to the shepherds a baby born in a manger. Not a sign of power, self-sufficiency or pride. No. The eternal God is reduced to a helpless, meek, humble human being. God lowered himself so that we could walk with him and so that he could stand beside us, not above and far from us.

Awe and wonder are the two feelings that move everyone, young and old, before the Nativity scene, which is like a living Gospel overflowing from the pages of Holy Scripture. It is not important how the Nativity scene is set up; it can always remain the same or change every year; what matters is that it speaks to life.

The first biographer of St. Francis, Thomas of Celano, describes the Christmas night of 1223, whose eight hundredth anniversary we celebrate this year. When Francis arrived, he found the crib with the hay, the ox and the donkey. Before the Christmas scene the people who flocked to the place manifested an unspeakable joy, never tasted before. Then the priest, at the manger, solemnly celebrated the Eucharist, showing the link between the Incarnation of the Son of God and the Eucharist. On that occasion, there were no figurines in Greccio: the Nativity scene was created and experienced by those who were present.

I am sure that the first Nativity scene, which accomplished a great work of evangelization, can also be an occasion today to summon forth awe and wonder. Thus, what the simplicity of that sign made St. Francis realize persists down to our own days as a genuine form of the beauty of our faith.

Vatican City, 27 September 2023

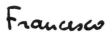

The Nativity Scene

And the day of joy is coming, the time of exultation! Many friars from various parts have been summoned here for the occasion; rejoicing men and women arrive from the farmhouses of the region, each one bringing, according to his possibilities, candles and torches to illuminate that night, in which the star that illuminated all days and times lit up splendidly in the sky. Francis arrives at the end: he sees that everything is arranged according to his desire, and he is radiant with joy. Now the crib is arranged, the hay is placed in it and the ox and the donkey are introduced. In that moving scene, evangelical simplicity shines, poverty is praised, humility is recommended. Greccio has become like a new Bethlehem.

Thomas of Celano, *The Crib of Greccio*

Who Is Happy in the Nativity Scene?

Let us look at the Nativity scene. Who is happy in the Nativity? I would like to ask you children, who love to look at the little figures ... and maybe even move them a bit, putting them in different places, angering your dad who arranged them with such care!

So, who is happy in the Nativity scene? Our Lady and Saint Joseph are full of joy: they look at the Child Jesus and they are happy because, after a thousand worries, they have accepted this gift of God, with so much faith and so much love. They are "overflowing" with holiness and therefore with joy. And you will tell me: of course! They are Our Lady and Saint Joseph! Yes, but let us not think it was easy for them: saints are not born, they become thus, and this is true for them too.

Then, the shepherds are full of joy. The shepherds too are holy, certainly, because they responded to the announcement of the angels; they immediately rushed to the stable and they recognized the sign of the Child in the manger. It was not obvious. In particular, in Nativity displays there is often a young shepherd, who looks toward the scene with a dreamy, enchanted air: that shepherd expresses the astonished joy of those who welcome the mystery of Jesus with a child's spirit. This is a trait of holiness: to preserve the capacity to be amazed, to wonder at the gifts of God, His "surprises," and the greatest gift, the ever-new surprise, is Jesus. The great surprise is God!

Then, in some Nativities, the bigger ones, with so many characters, there are the trades: the cobbler, the water trapper, the blacksmith, the baker ... and so on and so forth. And everyone is happy. Why? Because they are "infected" by the joy of the event in which they participate, that is, the birth of Jesus. So their work is also sanctified by the presence of Jesus, by His coming among us....

So my wish is this: to be holy, to be happy. But not picture-postcard saints! Normal saints. Saints in flesh and blood, with our character, our faults, even our sins—let us ask for forgiveness and go ahead—but ready to let ourselves be "infected" by Jesus' presence in our midst, ready to come to Him, like the shepherds, to see this Event, this incredible sign that God has given us. "I bring you good news that will cause great joy for all the people" (Lk 2:10). Will we go see Him? Or will we be occupied with things?

Saint Francis of Assisi, Who Invented the Nativity Scene

The enchanting image of the Christmas crèche, so dear to the Christian people, never ceases to arouse amazement and wonder. The depiction of Jesus' birth is itself a simple and joyful proclamation of the mystery of the Incarnation of the Son of God. The Nativity scene is like a living Gospel rising up from the pages of sacred Scripture. As we contemplate the Christmas story, we are invited to set out on a spiritual journey, drawn by the humility of the God who became man in order to encounter every man and woman. We come to realize that so great is his love for us that he became one of us, so that we in turn might become one with him.

I wish to encourage the beautiful family tradition of preparing the Nativity scene in the days before Christmas, but also the custom of setting it up in the workplace, in schools, hospitals, prisons, and town squares. Great imagination and creativity is always shown in employing the most diverse materials to create small masterpieces of beauty. As children, we learn from our parents and grandparents to carry on this joyful tradition, which encapsulates a wealth of popular piety. It is my hope that this custom will never be lost and that, wherever it has fallen into disuse, it can be rediscovered and revived.

The origin of the Christmas crèche is found above all in certain details of Jesus' birth in Bethlehem, as related in the Gospels. The evangelist Luke says simply that Mary "gave birth to her firstborn son and wrapped him in swaddling cloths, and laid him in a manger, because there was no place for them in the inn" (2:7). Because Jesus was laid in a manger, the Nativity scene is known in Italian as a *presepe*, from the Latin word *praesepium*, meaning "manger"….

But let us go back to the origins of the Christmas crèche so familiar to us. We need to imagine ourselves in the little Italian town of Greccio, near Rieti. Saint Francis stopped there, most likely on his way back from Rome, where on 29 November 1223 he had received the confirmation of his Rule from Pope Honorius III. Francis had earlier visited the Holy Land, and the caves in Greccio reminded him of the countryside of Bethlehem. It may also be that the "Poor Man of Assisi" had been struck by the mosaics in the Roman Basilica of Saint Mary Major depicting the birth of Jesus, close to the place where, according to an ancient tradition, the wooden panels of the manger are preserved.

The *Franciscan Sources* describe in detail what then took place in Greccio. Fifteen days before Christmas, Francis asked a local man named John to help him realize his desire "to bring to life the memory of that babe born in Bethlehem, to see as much as possible with my own bodily eyes the discomfort of his infant needs, how he lay in a manger, and how, with an ox and an ass standing by, he was laid upon a bed of hay." At this, his faithful friend went immediately to prepare all that the Saint had asked. On 25 December, friars came to Greccio from various parts, together with people from the farmsteads in the area, who brought flowers and torches to light up that holy night. When Francis arrived, he found a manger full of hay, an ox and a donkey. All those present experienced a new and indescribable joy in the presence of the Christmas scene. The priest then solemnly celebrated the Eucharist over the manger, showing the bond between the Incarnation of the Son of God and the Eucharist. At Greccio there were no statues; the Nativity scene was enacted and experienced by all who were present.

This is how our tradition began: with everyone gathered in joy around the cave, with no distance between the original event and those sharing in its mystery.

Thomas of Celano, the first biographer of Saint Francis, notes that this simple and moving scene was accompanied by the gift of a marvelous vision: one of those present saw the Baby Jesus himself lying in the manger. From the Nativity scene of that Christmas in 1223, "everyone went home with joy."

With the simplicity of that sign, Saint Francis carried out a great work of evangelization. His teaching touched the hearts of Christians and continues today to offer a simple yet authentic means of portraying the beauty of our faith. Indeed, the place where this first Nativity scene was enacted expresses and evokes these sentiments. Greccio has become a refuge for the soul, a mountain fastness wrapped in silence....

Setting up the Christmas crèche in our homes helps us to relive the history of what took place in Bethlehem. Naturally, the Gospels remain our source for understanding and reflecting on that event. At the same time, its portrayal in the crèche helps us to imagine the scene. It touches our hearts and makes us enter into salvation history as contemporaries of an event that is living and real in a broad gamut of historical and cultural contexts.

In a particular way, from the time of its Franciscan origins, the Nativity scene has invited us to "feel" and "touch" the poverty that God's Son took upon himself in the Incarnation. Implicitly, it summons us to follow him along the path of humility, poverty and self-denial that leads from the manger of Bethlehem to the cross. It asks us to meet him and serve him by showing mercy to those of our brothers and sisters in greatest need (cf. Mt 25:31-46)....

Standing before the Christmas crèche, we are reminded of the time when we were children, eagerly waiting to set it up. These memories make us all the more conscious of the precious gift received from those who passed on the faith to us. At the same time, they remind us of our duty to share this same experience with our children and our grandchildren. It does not matter how the Nativity scene is arranged: it can always be the same or it can change from year to year. What matters is that it speaks to our lives. Wherever it is, and whatever form it takes, the Christmas crèche speaks to us of the love of God, the God who became a child in order to make us know how close he is to every man, woman, and child, regardless of their condition.

The Nativity Scene Is Like a Living Gospel

It will be Christmas in one week. During these days as we rush to prepare for the feast day we can ask ourselves: "How am I preparing for the Birth of the celebrated One?" A simple, yet effective way to prepare oneself is to *set up a Nativity scene....*

Indeed, the Nativity scene is "like a living Gospel" (Apostolic Letter *Admirabile Signum*, n. 1). It brings the Gospel to the places where people live: in homes, schools, work and meeting places, hospitals, retirement homes, prisons, and in the squares. And in those places where we live, it reminds us of an essential thing: that God did not remain invisible in Heaven, but rather came to earth, became man, a child. To make a Nativity scene is *to celebrate God's closeness.* God has always been close to his people but when he became incarnate and was born, he was very close, extremely close. To make a Nativity scene is to celebrate God's closeness; to rediscover that God is real, concrete, alive and vibrant. God is not a distant lord or a detached judge but rather humble Love that descended upon us. The Child in the Nativity scene transmits his tenderness to us. Some small figurines portray the *"Bambinello"* with open arms to tell us that God came to embrace our humanity. It is beautiful then to stand before the Nativity scene and to confide our lives to the Lord, to speak to him of the people and situations that we have in our heart, to take stock with him of the year that is ending, to share our expectations and apprehensions.

We can see Mary and Joseph beside Jesus. We can guess the thoughts and feelings they had as the Babe was being born in poverty: joy but also dismay. And we can also invite the Holy Family into our homes where there are joys and worries, where we wake up each day, we eat and sleep close to the people who are dearest to us. The Nativity scene is a "*domestic Gospel.*" The word "*presepe*" (Nativity scene in Italian) literally means "manger" whereas Bethlehem, the town of the Nativity scene, means "house of bread." Manger and house of bread: the Nativity scene we set up at home where we share food and affection reminds us that Jesus is the nourishment, the bread of life (cf. Jn 6:34). He is the One who sustains our love. He is the One who gives our families the strength to carry on and forgive one another.

The Nativity scene offers us another life lesson. In today's at times frenetic pace, it is *an invitation to contemplation*. It reminds us of the importance of pausing. Because only when we know how to recollect ourselves can we welcome what truly matters in life. Only if we leave the din of the world outside our home can we open ourselves to listen to God who speaks in silence….

The Nativity scene is more timely now than ever, when every day, throughout the world, so many weapons and violent images that penetrate our eyes and hearts are being produced. The Nativity scene instead is an *artisanal image of peace*. This is why it is a living Gospel….

I hope that setting up the Nativity scene will be for you all an opportunity to invite Jesus into your lives. When we make the Nativity scene at home it is like opening a door and saying: "Come in, Jesus!" It is making this closeness concrete, this invitation to Jesus to come into our lives. Because if he abides in our lives, life is reborn. And if life is reborn, it is truly Christmas.

The Child Jesus

In those days Caesar Augustus issued a decree that a census should be taken of the entire Roman world. (This was the first census that took place while Quirinius was governor of Syria.) And everyone went to their own town to register.

So Joseph also went up from the town of Nazareth in Galilee to Judea, to Bethlehem the town of David, because he belonged to the house and line of David. He went there to register with Mary, who was pledged to be married to him and was expecting a child. While they were there, the time came for the baby to be born, and she gave birth to her firstborn, a son. She wrapped him in cloths and placed him in a manger, because there was no guest room available for them.

—Luke 2:1-7

As a Child God Baffles Us

When, at Christmas, we place the statue of the Infant Jesus in the manger, the Nativity scene suddenly comes alive. God appears as a child, for us to take into our arms. Beneath weakness and frailty, he conceals his power that creates and transforms all things. It seems impossible, yet it is true: in Jesus, God was a child, and in this way he wished to reveal the greatness of his love: by smiling and opening his arms to all.

The birth of a child awakens joy and wonder; it sets before us the great mystery of life. Seeing the bright eyes of a young couple gazing at their newborn child, we can understand the feelings of Mary and Joseph who, as they looked at the Infant Jesus, sensed God's presence in their lives....

God's ways are astonishing, for it seems impossible that he should forsake his glory to become a man like us. To our astonishment, we see God acting exactly as we do: he sleeps, takes milk from his mother, cries, and plays like every other child! As always, God baffles us. He is unpredictable, constantly doing what we least expect. The Nativity scene shows God as he came into our world, but it also makes us reflect on how our life is part of God's own life. It invites us to become his disciples if we want to attain ultimate meaning in life.

The Lord Offers Himself in Littleness

The Gospel ... relates the birth of Jesus beginning with Caesar Augustus, who orders the census of the whole world: it presents the first Emperor in all his *grandeur*. Yet immediately thereafter it brings us to Bethlehem, where there is no grandeur at all: just a poor child wrapped in swaddling clothes, with shepherds standing by. That is where God is, in *littleness*. This is the message: God does not rise up in grandeur, but lowers himself into littleness. Littleness is the path that he chose to draw near to us, to touch our hearts, to save us, and to bring us back to what really matters.

Brothers and sisters, standing before the crib, we contemplate what is central, beyond all the pretty lights and decorations. We contemplate the child. In his *littleness*, God is completely present. Let us acknowledge this: "Baby Jesus, you are God, the God who becomes a child." Let us be amazed by this scandalous truth. The

One who embraces the universe needs to be held in another's arms. The One who created the sun needs to be warmed. Tenderness incarnate needs to be coddled. Infinite love has a miniscule heart that beats softly. The eternal Word is an "infant," a speechless child. The Bread of life needs to be nourished. The Creator of the world has no home. Today, all is turned upside down: God comes into the world in littleness. His grandeur appears in *littleness*.

Let us ask ourselves: can we accept God's way of doing things? This is the challenge of Christmas: God reveals himself, but men and women fail to understand. He makes himself little in the eyes of the world, while we continue to seek grandeur in the eyes of the world, perhaps even in his name. God lowers himself and we try to become great. The Most High goes in search of shepherds, the unseen in our midst, and we look for visibility; we want to be seen. Jesus is born in order to serve, and we spend a lifetime pursuing success. God does not seek power and might; he asks for tender love and interior littleness.

This is what we should ask Jesus for at Christmas: *the grace of littleness*. "Lord, teach us to love littleness. Help us to understand that littleness is the way to authentic greatness." What does it mean, concretely, to accept littleness? In the first place, it is to believe that God desires to come *into the little things of our life*; he wants to inhabit our daily lives, the things we do each day at home, in our families, at school, and in the workplace. Amid our ordinary lived experience, he wants to do extraordinary things. His is a message of immense hope. Jesus asks us to rediscover and value the little things in life. If he is present there, what else do we need? Let us stop pining for a grandeur that is not ours to have. Let us put aside our complaints and our gloomy faces, and the greed that never satisfies! Littleness and the amazement of that little child: this is the message.

Yet there is more. Jesus does not want to come merely in the little things of our lives, but also *in our own littleness*: in our experience of feeling weak, frail, inadequate, perhaps even "messed up." Dear sister or brother, if, as in Bethlehem, the darkness of night overwhelms you, if you feel surrounded by cold indifference, if the hurt you carry inside cries out, "You are of little account; you are worthless; you will never be loved the way you want," tonight, if this is what you are feeling, God answers back. He tells you: "I love you just as you are. Your littleness does not frighten me, your failings do not trouble me. I became little for your sake. To be your God, I became your brother. Dear brother, dear sister, don't be afraid of me. Find in me your measure of greatness. I am close to you, and one thing only do I ask: trust me and open your heart to me."

To accept littleness means something else too. It means embracing Jesus *in the little ones of today*. Loving him, that is, in the least of our brothers and sisters. Serving him in the poor, those most like Jesus who was born in poverty. It is in them that he wants to be honored. On this night of love, may we have only one fear: that of offending God's love, hurting him by despising the poor with our indifference. Jesus loves them dearly, and one day they will welcome us to heaven. A poet once wrote: "Who has found not the heaven—below—Will fail of it above" (Emily Dickinson, *Poems*, P96-17). Let us not lose sight of heaven; let us care for Jesus now, caressing him in the needy, because in them he makes himself known.

Jesus, the Tenderness of God

In the face of little Jesus we contemplate the face of God, who does not reveal himself in strength and power but in the weakness and frailty of a newborn babe. This is what our God is like, he comes so close, in a child. This Child reveals the faithfulness and tenderness of the unconditional love with which God surrounds each one of us. That is why we celebrate at Christmas, thus reliving what the shepherds at Bethlehem experienced. And we celebrate together with so many fathers and mothers who struggle each day, facing so many sacrifices; we celebrate together with the little ones, the sick, the poor, for it is the celebration of God's encounter with us in Jesus.

A Child Is Born for Us

I would like to bring to everyone the message that the Church proclaims on this feast with the words of the prophet Isaiah: "To us a child is born, to us a son is given" (Is 9:6)

A child is born. A birth is always a source of hope; it is life that blossoms, a promise of the future. Moreover, this Child, Jesus, was born "to us": an "us" without any borders, privileges, or exclusions. The Child born of the Virgin Mary in Bethlehem was born for everyone: he is the "son" that God has given to the entire human family.

Thanks to this Child, all of us can speak to God and call him "Father." Jesus is the only begotten Son; no one but he knows the Father. Yet he came into the world for this very reason: to show us the face of the Father. Thanks to this Child, we can all call one another brothers and sisters, for so we truly are. We come from every continent, from every language and culture, with our own identities and differences, yet we are all brothers and sisters....

"To us a child is born" (Is 9:6). He came to save us! He tells us that pain and evil are not the final word. To become resigned to violence and injustice would be to reject the joy and hope of Christmas....

Jesus was born in a stable, but was embraced by the love of the Virgin Mary and Saint Joseph. By his birth in the flesh, the Son of God consecrated familial love. My thoughts at this moment turn to families: to those who cannot come together today and to those forced to remain at home. May Christmas be an opportunity for all of us to rediscover the family as a cradle of life and faith, a place of acceptance and love, dialogue, forgiveness, fraternal solidarity and shared joy, a source of peace for all humanity.

It Is the Feast of "For Us"

The birth of Jesus is the "newness" that enables us to be reborn each year and to find, in him, the strength needed to face every trial. Why? Because his birth is for us—for me, for you, for all of us, for everyone. *"For"* is a word that appears again and again on this holy night: *"For us* a child is born," Isaiah prophesied. *"For us* is born this day a Savior," we repeat in the Psalm. Jesus "gave himself *for us*" (Tit 2:14), Saint Paul tells us, and in the Gospel the angel proclaims: *"For to you* is born this day a Savior" (Lk 2:11). For me, for you.

Yet what do those words—*for us*—really mean? They mean that the Son of God, the one who is holy by nature, came to make us, as God's children, holy by grace. Yes, God came into the world as a child to make us children of God. What a magnificent gift! This day, God amazes us and says to each of us: "You are amazing." Dear sister, dear brother, never be discouraged. Are you tempted to feel you were a mistake? God tells you, "No, you are *my* child!" Do you have a feeling of failure or inadequacy, the fear that you will never emerge from the dark tunnel of trial? God says to you, "Have courage, I am with you." He does this not in words, but by making himself a child with you and for you. In this way, he reminds you that the starting point of all rebirth is the recognition that we are children of God. This is the starting point for any rebirth. This is the undying heart of our hope, the incandescent core that gives warmth and meaning to our life. Underlying all our strengths and weaknesses, stronger than all our past hurts and failures, or our fears and concerns about the future, there is this great truth: we are beloved sons and daughters. God's love for us does not, and never will, depend upon us. It is *completely free love*. Tonight cannot be explained in any other way: it is purely grace. Everything is grace. The gift is *completely free*, unearned by any of us, pure grace. Tonight, Saint Paul tells us, "the grace of God has appeared" (Tit 2:11). Nothing is more precious than this.

To us a son is given. The Father did not give us a thing, an object; he gave his own only begotten Son, who is all his joy. Yet if we look at our ingratitude toward God and our injustice toward so many of our brothers and sisters, a doubt can arise. Was the Lord right in giving us so much? Is he right still to trust us? Does he not overestimate us? Of course he overestimates us, and he does this because he is madly in love with us. He cannot help but love us. That is the way he is, so different from us. God always loves us with a greater love than we have for ourselves. This is his secret for entering our hearts. God knows that the only way to save us, to heal us from within, is by loving us: there is no other way. He knows that we become better only by accepting his *unfailing love*, an unchanging love that changes us. Only the love of Jesus can transform our life, heal our deepest hurts and set us free from the vicious circles of disappointment, anger, and constant complaint....

To us a son is given. Parents of little children know how much love and patience they require. We must feed them, look after them, bathe them, and care for their vulnerability and their needs, which are often difficult to understand. A child makes us feel loved but can also teach us how to love. God was born a child in order to encourage us to care for others. His quiet tears make us realize the uselessness of our many impatient outbursts; and we have so many of them! His disarming love reminds us that our time is not to be spent in feeling sorry for ourselves, but in comforting the tears of the suffering. God came among us in poverty and need, to tell us that in serving the poor, we will show our love for him. From this night onward, as a poet wrote, "God's residence is next to mine, his furniture is love" (Emily Dickinson, *Poems*, XVII).

To us a son is given. Jesus, you are the Child who makes me a child. You love me as I am, not as I imagine myself to be; this I know! In embracing you, the Child of the manger, I once more embrace my life. In welcoming you, the Bread of life, I too desire to give my life. You, my Savior, teach me to serve. You who did not leave me alone, help me to comfort your brothers and sisters, for you know that, from this night forward, all are my brothers and sisters.

✁

God Wants to Dwell in Us

The Gospel of today's Liturgy offers us a beautiful phrase that we always pray in the *Angelus* and which, on its own, reveals to us the meaning of Christmas. It says, "The Word became flesh and dwelt among us" (Jn 1:14). The Word became flesh and dwelt among us. If we think about it, these words contain a paradox. They bring together two opposing realities: the *Word* and the *flesh*. "Word" indicates that Jesus is the eternal Word of the Father, an infinite Word, existing from all time, before all created things; "flesh," on the other hand, indicates precisely our reality, a created, fragile, limited and mortal reality. Before Jesus there were two separate worlds: Heaven opposed to earth, the infinite opposed to the finite, spirit opposed to matter. And there is another polarity in the Prologue of the Gospel of John, another pair: *light* and *darkness* (cf. v. 5). Jesus is the light of God who has entered into the darkness of the world. *Light* and *darkness*. God is light: in him there is no opacity; in us, on the other hand, there is much darkness. Now, with Jesus, light and darkness meet: holiness and guilt, grace and sin. Jesus, the incarnation of Jesus, is the very place of encounter, the encounter between God and humanity, the encounter between grace and sin.

What does the Gospel intend to announce with these polarities? Something splendid: God's way of acting. Faced with our frailties, the Lord does not withdraw. He does not remain in his blessed eternity and in his infinite light, but rather he draws close, he makes himself flesh, he descends into the darkness, he dwells in lands that are foreign to him. And why does God do this? Why does he come down to us? He does this because he does not resign himself to the fact that we may lose our way, going far from him, far from eternity, far from the light. This is God's work: *to come among us*. If we consider ourselves unworthy, that does not stop him: he comes. If we reject him, he does not tire of seeking us out. If we are not ready and willing to receive him, he prefers to come anyway. And if we close the door in his face, he waits. He is truly the Good Shepherd. And [what is] the most beautiful image of the Good Shepherd? The Word that becomes flesh to share in our life. Jesus is the Good Shepherd who comes to seek us right where we are: in our problems, in our suffering.... He comes there....

We often keep our distance from God because we think we are not worthy of him for other reasons. And it is true. But Christmas invites us to see things *from his point of view*. God wishes to be incarnate. If your heart seems too contaminated by evil, if it seems untidy, please, do not close yourself up, do not be afraid: he will come. Think of the stable in Bethlehem. Jesus was born there, in that poverty, to tell us that he is certainly not afraid of visiting your heart, of dwelling in a shabby life. This is the word: to *dwell*. To *dwell* is the verb used in the Gospel to signify this reality: it expresses total sharing, a great intimacy. And this is what God wants: he wants to dwell *with* us, he wants to dwell *in* us, not to remain distant.

He Incarnated, And He Doesn't Go Back

Jesus is the Word, the eternal Word of God, who has always thought of us and wanted to communicate with us: this is the wondrous message of the Gospel.

And to do so, he went beyond words. In fact, at the heart of today's Gospel we are told that "the Word became flesh and dwelt among us" (v. 14). The Word became *flesh*: why does Saint John use this expression "flesh"? Could he not have said, in a more elegant way, that the Word was made *man*? No, he uses the word flesh because it indicates our human condition in all its weakness, in all its frailty. He tells us that God became fragile so he could touch our fragility up close. Thus, from the moment the Lord became flesh, nothing about our life is extraneous to him. There is nothing that he scorns; we can share everything with him, everything. Dear brother, dear sister, God became flesh to tell us, to tell you that he loves you right there, that he loves us right there, in our frailties, in your frailties; right there, where we are most ashamed, where you are most ashamed. This is bold, God's decision is bold: He became flesh precisely where very often we are ashamed; He enters into our shame, to become our brother, to share the path of life.

He became flesh and never turned back. He did not put on our humanity like a garment that can be put on and taken off. No, he never detached himself from our flesh. And he will never be separated from it: now and forever he is in heaven with his body made of human flesh. He has united himself forever to our humanity; we might say that he "espoused" himself to it. I like to think that when the Lord prays to the Father for us, he does not merely speak: he shows him the wounds of the flesh, he shows him the wounds he suffered for us. This is Jesus: with his flesh he is the intercessor; he wants to bear even the signs of suffering. Jesus, with his flesh, is before the Father. Indeed, the Gospel says that *He came to dwell among us.* He did not come to visit us, and then leave; He came to dwell with us, to stay with us. What, then, does he desire from us? He desires a great intimacy. He wants us to share with him our joys and sufferings, desires and fears, hopes and sorrows, people and situations. Let us do this, with confidence: let us open our hearts to him, let us tell him everything. Let us pause in silence before the Nativity scene to savor the tenderness of God who became near, who became flesh. And without fear, let us invite him among us, into our homes, into our families. And also—everyone knows this well—let us invite him into our frailties. Let us invite him, so that he may see our wounds. He will come and life will change.

At Christmas, God Sided with Man

And the reason for our hope is this: God is with us and God still trusts us! Think well on this: God is with us and God still trusts us. God the Father is generous. He comes to abide with mankind. He chooses earth as his dwelling place to remain with people and to be found where man passes his days in joy or in sorrow. Therefore, earth is no longer only "a valley of tears"; rather, it is the place where God himself has pitched his tent. It is the meeting place of God with man, of God's solidarity with men.

God willed to share in our human condition to the point of becoming one with us in the Person of Jesus, who is true Man and true God. However, there is something even more surprising.

The presence of God among men did not take place in a perfect, idyllic world but rather in this real world, which is marked by so many things both good and bad, by division, wickedness, poverty, arrogance, and war. He chose to live in our history as it is, with all the weight of its limitations and of its tragedies. In doing so, he has demonstrated in an unequalled manner his merciful and truly loving disposition toward the human creature. He is God-with-us. Jesus is God-with-us. Do you believe this? Together let us profess: Jesus is God with us! Jesus is God with us always and forever, with us in history's suffering and sorrow. The Birth of Jesus reveals that God "sided" with man once and for all, to save us, to raise us from the dust of our misery, from our difficulty, from our sins.

Hence the great "gift" of the Child of Bethlehem: He brings us a spiritual energy, an energy which helps us not to despair in our struggle, in our hopelessness, in our sadness, for it is an energy that warms and transforms the heart. Indeed, the Birth of Jesus brings us the good news that we are loved immensely and uniquely by God, and he not only enables us to know this love, he also gives it to us, he communicates it to us!

We may derive two considerations from the joyous contemplation of the mystery of the Son of God born for us.

The first is that if God, in the Christmas mystery, reveals himself not as One who remains on high and dominates the universe, but as the One who bends down, descends to the little and poor earth, it means that, to be like him, we should not put ourselves above others, but indeed lower ourselves, place ourselves at the service of others, become small with the small and poor with the poor. It is regrettable to see a Christian who does not want to lower himself, who does not want to serve. A Christian who struts about is ugly: this is not Christian, it is pagan. The Christian serves, he lowers himself. Let us be sure that our brothers and sisters do not ever feel alone!

The second consequence: if God, through Jesus, involved himself with man to the point of becoming one of us, it means that whatever we have done to a brother or a sister we have done to him. Jesus himself reminded us of this: whoever has fed, welcomed, visited, loved one of the least and poorest of men, will have done it to the Son of God.

Let us entrust ourselves to the maternal intercession of Mary, the Mother of Jesus and our Mother, that she may help us this holy Christmastide, which is already close at hand, to see in the face of our neighbor, especially the weakest and most marginalized people, the image of the Son of God made man.

The Child Jesus is God's Smile

The Virgin and her husband, with their love, made a smile blossom on the lips of their newborn child. But when this happened, their hearts were filled with a new joy, from Heaven. And the little stable in Bethlehem was illuminated.

Jesus is the smile of God. He came to reveal to us the love of our Heavenly Father, His goodness, and the first way He did so was to smile at His parents, like every newborn child in this world. And they, the Virgin Mary and Saint Joseph, because of their great faith, were able to accept that message. They recognized in Jesus' smile God's mercy for them and for all those who were waiting for His coming, the coming of the Messiah, the Son of God, the King of Israel.

Behold, in the manger we too relive this experience: to look at the Child Jesus and feel that God is smiling at us there, and smiling at all the poor of the earth, at all those who await salvation, who hope for a more fraternal world, where there is no more war and violence, where every man and woman can live in his or her dignity as son and daughter of God....

We always need to let ourselves be renewed by the smile of the Child Jesus. Let His defenseless goodness purify us from the waste that often encrusts our hearts, and prevents us from giving the best of ourselves....

Sometimes it becomes difficult to smile, for many reasons. Then we need God's smile: Jesus, only He can help us. Only He is the Savior, and sometimes we experience this in our lives.

Other times things go well, but then there is the danger of feeling too safe and forgetting about others who are struggling. Then too we need God's smile to strip us of false security and bring us back to the taste for simplicity and gratuitousness.

Let us exchange this wish: at Christmas, participating in the Liturgy, and also contemplating the manger, let us wonder at God's smile, which Jesus came to bring. It is He Himself, this smile. Like Mary, like Joseph and the shepherds of Bethlehem, let us welcome Him, let us allow ourselves to be purified, and we too can bring others a humble, simple smile.

Thank you all! Take this wish to your loved ones at home, especially the sick and the elderly.

The Grace of Tenderness

The Child in the Nativity scene transmits his tenderness to us. Some small figurines portray the "*Bambinello*" with open arms to tell us that God came to embrace our humanity. It is beautiful then to stand before the Nativity scene and to confide our lives to the Lord, to speak to him of the people and situations that we have in our heart, to take stock with him of the year that is ending, to share our expectations and apprehensions.

Let the Lord Come and Find Us

On this holy night, while we contemplate the Infant Jesus just born and placed in the manger, we are invited to reflect. How do we welcome the tenderness of God? Do I allow myself to be taken up by God, to be embraced by him, or do I prevent him from drawing close? "But I am searching for the Lord"— we could respond. Nevertheless, what is most important is not seeking him, but rather allowing him to seek me, find me, and caress me with tenderness. The question put to us simply by the Infant's presence is: do I allow God to love me?

More so, do we have the courage to welcome with tenderness the difficulties and problems of those who are near to us, or do we prefer impersonal solutions, perhaps effective but devoid of the warmth of the Gospel? How much the world needs tenderness today! The patience of God, the closeness of God, the tenderness of God.

The Christian response cannot be different from God's response to our smallness. Life must be met with goodness, with meekness. When we realize that God is in love with our smallness, that he made himself small in order to better encounter us, we cannot help but open our hearts to him, and beseech him: "Lord, help me to be like you, give me the grace of tenderness in the most difficult circumstances of life, give me the grace of closeness in the face of every need, of meekness in every conflict."

What Children Teach Us

There was a time in which, in the divine-human Person of Christ, God was a child, and this must hold a particular significance for our faith. It is true that his death on the cross and his Resurrection are the highest expressions of his redeeming love, however let us not forget that the whole of his earthly life is revelation and teaching. In the Christmas season we remember his childhood. In order to grow in faith, we will need to contemplate the Child Jesus more often. Certainly, we know nothing of this period of his life. The rare indications that we possess refer to the imposition of his name eight days after his birth and his presentation at the Temple (cf. Lk 2:21-28); in addition to this, the visit of the Magi and the ensuing escape to Egypt (cf. Mt 2:1-23). Then, there is a great leap to twelve years of age, when with Mary and Joseph he goes in pilgrimage to Jerusalem for Passover, and instead of returning with his parents, he remains in the Temple to speak with the doctors of the law.

As we see, we know little of the Child Jesus, but we can learn much about him if we look to the lives of children. It is a beautiful habit that parents and grandparents have, that of watching what the children do.

We discover, first of all, that children want our attention. They have to be at the center—why? Because they are proud? No! Because they need to feel protected. It is important that we too place Jesus at the center of our life and know, even if it may seem paradoxical, that it is our responsibility to protect him. He wants to be in our embrace, he wants to be tended to and to be able to fix his gaze on ours. Additionally, we must make the Child Jesus smile in order to show him our love and our joy that he is in our midst. His smile is a sign of the love that gives us the assurance of being loved. Children, lastly, love to play. Playing with children, however, means abandoning our logic in order to enter theirs. If we want to have fun, it is necessary to understand what they like, and not to be selfish and make them do the things that we like. It is a lesson for us. Before Jesus we are called to abandon our pretense of autonomy—and this is the crux of the matter: our pretense of autonomy—in order to instead accept the true form of liberty, which consists in knowing and serving whom we have before us. He, the Child, is the Son of God who comes to save us. He has come among us to show us the face of the Father abounding in love and mercy. Therefore, let us hold the Child Jesus tightly in our arms; let us place ourselves at his service. He is the font of love and serenity. It will be beautiful today, when we get home, to go to the Nativity scene and kiss the Baby Jesus and say: "Jesus, I want to be humble like you, humble like God," and to ask him for this grace.

Seeing Jesus in the Little Excluded Ones

Today, as the winds of war are blowing in our world and an outdated model of development continues to produce human, societal, and environmental decline, Christmas invites us to focus on the sign of the Child and to recognize him in the faces of little children, especially those for whom, like Jesus, "there is no place in the inn" (Lk 2:7)....

We see Jesus in the children worldwide wherever peace and security are threatened by the danger of tensions and new conflicts....

We see Jesus in the children of unemployed parents who struggle to offer their children a secure and peaceful future. And in those whose childhood has been robbed and who, from a very young age, have been forced to work or to be enrolled as soldiers by unscrupulous mercenaries.

We see Jesus in the many children forced to leave their countries to travel alone in inhumane conditions and who become an easy target for human traffickers.... Jesus knows well the pain of not being welcomed and how hard it is not to have a place to lay one's head. May our hearts not be closed as they were in the homes of Bethlehem.

The sign of Christmas has also been revealed to us: "a baby wrapped in swaddling clothes" (Lk 2:12). Like the Virgin Mary and Saint Joseph, like the shepherds of Bethlehem, may we welcome in the Baby Jesus the love of God made man for us. And may we commit ourselves, with the help of his grace, to making our world more humane and more worthy for the children of today and of the future.

The Sign of a Newborn

The Child Jesus, born in Bethlehem, is the *sign* given by God to those who awaited salvation, and he remains forever the sign of God's tenderness and presence in our world. The angel announces to the shepherds: "This will be a sign for you: you will find a child...."

Today too, *children are a sign*. They are a sign of hope, a sign of life, but also a *"diagnostic" sign*, a marker indicating the health of families, society and the entire world. Wherever children are accepted, loved, cared for, and protected, the family is healthy, society is healthier, and the world is more humane....

To us, the men and women of the twenty-first century, God today also says: "This will be a sign for you," look to the child...

The Child of Bethlehem is frail, like all newborn children. He cannot speak and yet he is the Word made flesh who came to transform the hearts and lives of all men and women. This Child, like every other child, is vulnerable; he needs to be accepted and protected. Today too, children need to be welcomed and defended, from the moment of their conception.

Sadly, in this world, with all its highly developed technology, great numbers of children continue to live in inhumane situations, on the fringes of society, in the peripheries of great cities and in the countryside. All too many children continue to be exploited, maltreated, enslaved, prey to violence and illicit trafficking. Still too many children live in exile, as refugees, at times lost at sea, particularly in the waters of the Mediterranean. Today, in acknowledging this, we feel shame before God, before God who became a child.

And we have to ask ourselves: Who are we, as we stand before the Child Jesus? Who are we, as we stand before today's children? Are we like Mary and Joseph, who welcomed Jesus and cared for him with the love of a father and a mother? Or are we like Herod, who wanted to eliminate him? Are we like the shepherds, who went in haste to kneel before him in worship and offer him their humble gifts? Or are we indifferent? Are we perhaps people who use fine and pious words, yet exploit pictures of poor children in order to make money? Are we ready to be there for children, to "waste time" with them? Are we ready to listen to them, to care for them, to pray for them and with them? Or do we ignore them because we are too caught up in our own affairs?

"This will be a sign for us: you will find a child...." Perhaps that little boy or girl is crying. He is crying because he is hungry, because she is cold, because he or she wants to be picked up and held in our arms... Today too, children are crying, they are crying a lot, and their crying challenges us. In a world which daily discards tons of food and medicine, there are children, hungry and suffering from easily curable diseases, who cry out in vain. In an age which insists on the protection of minors, there is a flourishing trade in weapons which end up in the hands of child-soldiers, there is a ready market for goods produced by the slave labor of small children. Their cry is stifled: the cry of these children is stifled! They must fight, they must work, they cannot cry! But their mothers cry for them, as modern-day Rachels: they weep for their children, and they refuse to be consoled (cf. Mt 2:18).

"This will be a sign for you": you will find a child. The Child Jesus, born in Bethlehem, every child who is born and grows up in every part of our world, is a diagnostic sign indicating the state of health of our families, our communities, our nation. Such a frank and honest diagnosis can lead us to a new kind of lifestyle where our relationships are no longer marked by conflict, oppression, and consumerism, but fraternity, forgiveness, and reconciliation, solidarity and love.

God Is Born for Free

But we can still ask ourselves: why does Saint Paul describe the coming of God into our world as "grace"? To tell us that it is utterly free. Whereas on earth everything seems to be about giving in order to get, God comes down freely. His love is non-negotiable: we did nothing to deserve it and we will never be able to repay it.

The grace of God has appeared. Tonight we realize that, when we failed to measure up, God became small for our sake; while we were going about our own business, he came into our midst. Christmas reminds us that God continues to love us all, even the worst of us. To me, to you, to each of us, he says today: "I love you and I will always love you, for you are precious in my eyes."

God does not love you because you think and act the right way. He loves you, plain and simple. His love is unconditional; it does not depend on you. You may have mistaken ideas, you may have made a complete mess of things, but the Lord continues to love you. How often do we think that God is good if we are good and punishes us if we are bad. Yet that is not how he is. For all our sins, he continues to love us. His love does not change. It is not fickle; it is faithful. It is patient. This is the gift we find at

Christmas. We discover to our amazement that the Lord is absolute gratuity, absolute tender love. His glory does not overwhelm us; his presence does not terrify us. He is born in utter poverty in order to win our hearts by the wealth of his love.

The grace of God has appeared. Grace is a synonym of beauty. Tonight, in the beauty of God's love, we also discover our own beauty, for we are *beloved of God*. For better or worse, in sickness and in health, whether happy or sad, in his eyes we are beautiful, not for what we do but for what we are. Deep within us, there is an indelible and intangible beauty, an irrepressible beauty, which is the core of our being. Today God reminds us of this. He lovingly takes upon himself our humanity and makes it his own, "espousing" it forever....

What are we to do with this grace? Only one thing: *accept the gift*. Before we go out to seek God, let us allow ourselves to be sought by him. He always seeks us first. Let us not begin with our own abilities but with his grace, for he, Jesus, is the Savior. Let us contemplate the Child and let ourselves be caught up in his tender love. Then we have no further excuse for not letting ourselves be loved by him. Whatever goes wrong in our lives, whatever doesn't work in the Church, whatever problems there are in the world, will no longer serve as an excuse. It will become secondary, for faced with Jesus' extravagant love, a love of utter meekness and closeness, we have no excuse. At Christmas, the question is this: "Do I allow myself to be loved by God? Do I abandon myself to his love that comes to save me?"

So great a gift deserves immense gratitude. To accept this grace means to be ready to *give thanks in return*. Often we live our lives with such little gratitude. Today is the right day to draw near to the tabernacle, the crèche, the manger, and to say thank you. Let us receive the gift that is Jesus, in order then to *become gift* like Jesus. To become gift is to give meaning to life. And it is the best way to change the world....

Jesus shows this to us tonight. He did not change history by pressuring anyone or by a flood of words, but by the gift of his life. He did not wait until we were good before he loved us, but gave himself freely to us. May we not wait for our neighbors to be good before we do good to them, for the Church to be perfect before we love her, for others to respect us before we serve them. Let us begin with ourselves. This is what it means freely to accept the gift of grace. And holiness is nothing other than preserving this freedom.

Mary

But the angel said to her, "Do not be afraid, Mary; you have found favor with God.

—Luke 1:30

Born of Woman

Mary "gave birth to her firstborn son and wrapped him in bands of cloth, and laid him in a manger, because there was no place for them in the inn" (Lk 2:7). In these plain and clear words, Luke brings us to the heart of that holy night: Mary *gave birth*; she gave us Jesus, the *Light* of the world. A simple story that plunges us into the event that changes our history forever. Everything, that night, became a source of hope.

Let us go back a few verses. By decree of the Emperor, Mary and Joseph found themselves forced to set out. They had to leave their people, their home, and their land, and to undertake a journey in order to be registered in the census. This was no comfortable or easy journey for a young couple about to have a child: they had to leave their land. At heart, they were full of hope and expectation because of the child about to be born; yet their steps were weighed down by the uncertainties and dangers that attend those who must leave their home behind.

Then they found themselves having to face perhaps the most difficult thing of all. They arrived in Bethlehem and experienced that it was a land that was not expecting them. A land where there was no place for them.

And there, where everything was a challenge, Mary gave us Emmanuel.

There Is No Salvation Without Woman

"But when the time had fully come, God sent forth his Son, born of woman" (Gal 4:4). Born of woman: Jesus came in this way. He did not appear in the world as an adult but, as the Gospel tells us, he was "conceived in the womb" (Lk 2:21). It was there that he made our humanity his own: day after day, month after month. In the womb of a woman, God and mankind are united, never to be separated again. Even now, in heaven, Jesus lives in the flesh that he took in his mother's womb. In God, there is our human flesh!

We celebrate this nuptial union between God and mankind, inaugurated in the womb of a woman. In God, there will forever be our humanity and Mary will forever be the Mother of God. She is both woman and mother: this is what is essential. From her, a woman, salvation came forth and thus there is no salvation without a woman. In her, God was united to us, and if we want to unite ourselves to him, we must take the same path: through Mary, woman and mother. That is why we begin the year by celebrating Our Lady, the woman who wove the humanity of God. If we want to weave humanity into this our time, we need to start again from the woman.

Born of woman. The rebirth of humanity began from a woman. Women are sources of life. Yet they are continually insulted, beaten, raped, forced to prostitute themselves, and to suppress the life they bear in the womb. Every form of violence inflicted upon a woman is a blasphemy against God, who was born of a woman. Humanity's salvation came forth from the body of a woman: we can understand our degree of humanity by how we treat a woman's body. How often are women's bodies sacrificed on the profane altars of advertising, of profiteering, of pornography, exploited like a canvas to be used. Yet women's bodies must be freed from consumerism; they must be respected and honored. Theirs is the most noble flesh in the world, for it conceived and brought to light the love that has saved us! In our day, too, motherhood is demeaned, because the only growth that interests us is economic growth. There are mothers who risk difficult journeys desperately seeking to give a better future to the fruit of their womb, yet are deemed redundant by people with full stomachs but hearts empty of love....

Born of woman. Jesus, newly born, was mirrored in the eyes of the woman, in the face of his mother. From her, he received his first caresses; with her, he exchanged the first smiles. With her began the revolution of tenderness. The Church, looking at the Baby Jesus, is called to continue that revolution. For she too, like Mary, is both woman and mother. The Church is woman and mother, and in Our Lady, she finds her distinctive traits. She sees Mary immaculate, and feels called to say no to sin and to worldliness. She sees Mary fruitful, and feels called to proclaim the Gospel and to give birth to it in people's lives. She sees Mary a mother, and she feels called to receive every man and woman as a son or daughter.

Mary, or God Is within Our Reach

Let us imagine Mary who, as a tender and caring mother, has just laid Jesus in the manger. In that act of laying him down we can see a gift given to us: Our Lady does not just keep her Son to herself, but presents him to us. She does not just hold him in her arms, but puts him down to invite us to look at him, to welcome him and to adore him. This is Mary's motherhood: she offers the Son who is born to all of us. Always by giving her Son, showing her Son, never treating her Son as something of her own, no. And so throughout Jesus' life.

And in laying him before our eyes, without saying a word, she gives us a wonderful message: God is near, within our reach. He does not come with the power of one who wants to be feared, but with the frailness of someone who asks to be loved. He does not judge from his throne on high, but looks at us from below, like a brother, rather, like a son. He is born little and in need so that no one would ever again be ashamed of themselves. It is precisely when we experience our weakness and our frailness that we can feel God even nearer, because he appeared to us in this way—weak and frail. He is the God-child who is born so as not to exclude anyone, in order to make us all become brothers and sisters....

God who, in the arms of his mother and lying in a manger, encourages us with tenderness. We need this encouragement. We are still living in uncertain and difficult times due to the pandemic. Many are frightened about the future and burdened by social problems, personal problems, dangers stemming from the ecological crisis, injustices, and by global economic imbalances. Looking at Mary with her Son in her arms, I think of young mothers and their children fleeing wars and famine, or waiting in refugee camps. They are many! And while contemplating Mary who lays Jesus in the manger, making him available to everyone, let us remember that the world can change and everyone's life can improve only if we make ourselves available to others, without expecting them to begin to do so. If we become artisans of fraternity, we will be able to mend the threads of a world torn apart by war and violence.

Saying Yes to the Lord

"Rejoice" says the angel to Mary, "you will conceive in your womb and bear a son, and you shall call his name Jesus" (Lk 1:28, 31). It seems to be an announcement of pure joy, destined to make the Virgin happy. Who among the women of that time, did not dream of becoming the mother of the Messiah? But along with joy, those words foretell a great trial to Mary. Why? Because at that time she was "betrothed" (v. 27).

In such cases, the Law of Moses stated that there should be no relations or cohabitation. Therefore, by having a son, Mary would have transgressed the Law, and the punishment for women was terrible: stoning (cf. Dt 22:20-21). Certainly, the divine message would have filled Mary's heart with light and strength; nevertheless, she found herself faced with a crucial decision: to say "yes" to God, risking everything, even her life, or to decline the invitation and continue along her ordinary journey.

What does she do? She responds thus: "Let it be to me according to your word" (Lk 1:38). *"Let it be"* (*"Fiat"*). But in the language in which the Gospel is written, it is not simply "let it be." The verbal expression indicates a strong desire; it indicates the will that something happen. In other words, Mary does not say: "If it has to happen, let it happen..., if it cannot be otherwise...." It is not resignation. She does not express a weak and submissive acceptance, but rather she expresses a strong desire, a sincere desire. She is not passive, she is active. She does not defer to God, she cleaves to God. She is a woman in love prepared to serve her Lord completely and immediately. She could have asked for a little time to think it over, or even for more explanations about what would happen; perhaps she could have set some conditions.... Instead, she does not take her time, she does not keep God waiting, she does not delay.

How often—let us think of ourselves now—how often our life is made up of postponements, even the spiritual life! For example, I know it is good for me to pray, but today I do not have time ... "tomorrow, tomorrow, tomorrow, tomorrow." We postpone things: I will do it tomorrow. I know it is important to help someone—yes, I must do it: I will do it tomorrow. It is the same chain of tomorrows ... postponing things. Today, on the threshold of Christmas, Mary invites us not to postpone, to say "yes": "Do I have to pray?—Yes"—and I pray. "Do I have to help others?—Yes." "How shall I do it?"—I do it. Without putting it off. Every "yes" costs something; every "yes" has its cost, but it still costs less than what that courageous "yes" cost her, that prompt "yes," that "*let it be to me according to your word,*" which brought us salvation.

Mary Recognizes God's Time

Let us fix our gaze on this simple girl from Nazareth, at the moment she offers herself to the divine message with her "yes"; let us grasp two essential aspects of her attitude, which is for us the model of how to prepare for Christmas.

First of all her *faith*, her attitude of faith, which consists in listening to the Word of God in order to abandon herself to this Word with full willingness of mind and heart. Responding to the angel, Mary said: "Behold, I am the handmaid of the Lord; let it be to me according to your word" (v. 38). In her "behold" filled with faith, Mary does not know by what road she must venture, what pains she must suffer, what risks she must face. But she is aware that it is the Lord asking and she entrusts herself totally to Him; she abandons herself to his love. This is the faith of Mary!

Another aspect is the capacity of the Mother of Christ to *recognize God's time*. Mary is the one who made possible the Incarnation of the Son of God, "the revelation of the mystery which was kept secret for long ages" (Rom 16:25). She made possible the Incarnation of the Word thanks to her humble and brave "yes." Mary teaches us to seize the right moment when Jesus comes into our life and asks for a ready and generous answer. And Jesus is coming. Indeed, the mystery of the birth of Jesus in Bethlehem took place historically more than 2,000 years ago but occurs as a spiritual event in the "today" of the Liturgy. The Word, who found a home in the virgin womb of Mary, comes in the celebration of Christmas to knock once again at the heart of every Christian. He comes and knocks. Each of us is called to respond, like Mary, with a personal and sincere "yes," placing oneself fully at the disposal of God and of his mercy, of his love. How many times Jesus comes into our lives, and how many times he sends us an angel, and how many times we don't notice because we are so taken, immersed in our own thoughts, in our own affairs and even, in these days, in our Christmas preparations, so as not to notice Him who comes and knocks at the door of our hearts, asking for acceptance, asking for a "yes" like Mary's. A saint used to say: "I am afraid that the Lord will come." Do you know what the fear was? It was the fear of not noticing and letting Him pass by. When we feel in our hearts: "I would like to be a better man, a better woman…. I regret what I have done…." That is the Lord knocking. He makes you feel this: the will to be better, the will to be closer to others, to God. If you feel this, stop. That is the Lord! And go to prayer, and maybe to confession, cleanse yourselves… this will be good. But keep well in mind: if you feel this longing to be better, He is knocking: don't let Him pass by!

With Mary, the Lord Changes the Destiny of Humanity

Mary is presented in the light of the prophet who says: "Behold, a virgin shall conceive and bear a son" (v. 23). Matthew the Evangelist recognizes that this happened in Mary, who conceived Jesus through the Holy Spirit (cf. v. 18). The Son of God "comes" into her womb in order to become man, and she welcomes him. Thus, in a unique way, God drew near to mankind, taking on flesh through a woman: God drew near to us and took on flesh through a woman. To us too, in a different way, God draws near with his grace in order to enter our life and offer us the gift of his Son. What do we do? Do we welcome him, let him draw near, or do we reject him, push him away? As Mary, freely offering herself to the Lord of history, allowed him to change the destiny of mankind, so too can we, by welcoming Jesus and seeking to follow him each day, cooperate in his salvific plan for us and for the world. Mary thus appears to us as a model to look to and upon whose support we can count on in our search for God, in our closeness to God, in thus allowing God to draw close to us, and in our commitment to build the culture of love.

The Generative Faith of Mary

Mary, the Holy Mother of God, had to endure "the scandal of the manger." She too, long before the shepherds, had received the message of an angel, who spoke to her solemnly about the throne of David: "You will conceive in your womb and bear a son, and you will name him Jesus. He will be great, and will be called the Son of the Most High, and the Lord God will give to him the throne of his ancestor David" (Lk 1:31-32). And now, Mary has to lay him in a trough for animals. How can she hold together the throne of a king and the lowly manger? How can she reconcile the glory of the Most High and the bitter poverty of a stable? Let us think of the distress of the Mother of God. What can be more painful for a mother than to see her child suffering poverty? It is troubling indeed. We would not blame Mary, were she to complain of those unexpected troubles. Yet she does not lose heart. She does not complain, but keeps silent. Rather than complain, she chooses a different part: *For her part*, the Gospel tells us, Mary "kept all these things, pondering them in her heart" (cf. Lk 2:19).

That is not what the shepherds and the people do. The shepherds tell everyone about what they had seen: the angel that appeared in the heart of the night, and his words concerning the Child. And the people, upon hearing these things, are amazed (cf. v. 18). Words and amazement. Mary, instead, is pensive; she keeps all these things, pondering them in her heart. We ourselves can have the same two different responses. The story told by the shepherds, and their own amazement, remind us of the beginnings of faith, when everything seems easy and straightforward. We rejoice in the newness of God who enters into our lives and fills us with wonder. Mary's pensiveness, on the other hand, is the expression of a mature, adult faith, not a faith of beginners. Not a newborn faith, it is rather a faith that now *gives birth*. For spiritual fruitfulness is born of trials and testing. From the quiet of Nazareth and from the triumphant promises received by the angel—the beginnings—Mary now finds herself in the dark stable of Bethlehem. Yet that is where she gives God to the world. Others, before the scandal of the manger, might feel deeply troubled. She does not: she keeps those things, pondering them in her heart.

Let us learn from the Mother of God how to have that same attitude: to *keep* and to *ponder*. Because we may well have to endure certain "scandals of the manger." We hope that everything will be all right and then, like a bolt from the blue, an unexpected problem arises. Our expectations clash painfully with reality. That can also happen in the life of faith, when the joy of the Gospel is put to the test in troubling situations. Today the Mother of God teaches us to draw profit from this clash. She shows us that it is necessary: it is the narrow path to achieve the goal, the cross, without which there can be no resurrection. Like the pangs of childbirth, it begets a more mature faith.

How do we make this passage, how do we surmount this clash between the ideal and the real? By doing exactly what Mary did: by keeping and by pondering. First, Mary "keeps," that is she holds on to what happens; she does not forget or reject it.

She keeps in her heart everything that she saw and heard. The beautiful things, like those spoken to her by the angel and the shepherds, but also the troubling things: the danger of being found pregnant before marriage and, now, the lowly stable where she has had to give birth. That is what Mary does. She does not pick and choose; she *keeps*. She accepts life as it comes, without trying to camouflage or embellish it; she keeps those things in her heart.

Then, Mary's second attitude is about how she *keeps*: she keeps and she *ponders*. The Gospel speaks of Mary "bringing together," comparing her different experiences and finding the hidden threads that connect them. In her heart, in her prayer, she does exactly that: she binds together the beautiful things and the unpleasant things. She does not keep them apart, but brings them together. It is for this reason that Mary is said to be the Mother of Catholicity. In this regard, we can dare to say that it is because of this that Mary is said to be Catholic, for she unites, she does not divide. And in this way she discerns their greater meaning, from God's perspective. In her mother's heart, Mary comes to realize that the glory of the Most High appears in humility; she welcomes the plan of salvation whereby God must lie in a manger. She sees the divine Child frail and shivering, and she accepts the wondrous divine interplay between grandeur and littleness.

Mary Gives Us the Joy of Jesus

The Gospel of the Liturgy of today, fourth Sunday of Advent, tells of Mary's visit to Elizabeth (cf. Lk 1:39-45). After receiving the annunciation of the angel, the Virgin does not stay at home, thinking over what has happened and considering the problems and pitfalls, which were certainly not lacking: because, poor girl, she did not know what to do with this news, with the culture of that age… She did not understand…. On the contrary, she first thinks of someone in need; instead of being absorbed in her own problems, she thinks about someone in need, she thinks about Elizabeth, her relative, who was advanced in years and with child, something strange and miraculous. Mary sets out with generosity, without letting herself be daunted by the discomforts of the journey, responding to an inner impulse that called her to be close and to help. A long road, mile after mile, and no bus went there: she had to go on foot. She went out to help, sharing her joy. Mary gives Elizabeth the joy of Jesus, the joy she carried in her heart and in her womb. She goes to her and proclaims her feelings, and this proclamation of feelings then becomes a prayer, the *Magnificat*, which we all know. And the text says that Our Lady "arose and went with haste" (v. 39).

She *arose and went….* Let us be guided by these two verbs. To *arise* and to *go in haste*: these are the two movements that Mary made and that she also invites us to make as Christmas approaches. First of all, *arise*. After the angel's annunciation, a difficult period loomed ahead for the Virgin: her unexpected pregnancy exposed her to misunderstandings and even severe punishment, including stoning, in the culture of that time. Let us imagine how many concerns and worries she had! Nevertheless, she did not become discouraged, she was not disheartened: but she arose. She did not look down at her problems, but up to God. And she did not think about who to ask for help, but to whom to bring help. She always thought about others: that is Mary, always thinking of the needs of others. She would do the same later, at the wedding in Cana, when she realizes that there is no more wine. It is a problem for other people, but she thinks about this and tries to find a solution. Mary always thinks about others. She also thinks of us.

Let us learn this way of reacting from Our Lady: to arise, especially when difficulties threaten to crush us. To arise, so as not to get bogged down in problems, sinking into self-pity or falling into a sadness that paralyses us. But why get up? Because

God is great and is ready to lift us up again if we reach out to him. So let us cast to him the negative thoughts, the fears that block every impulse and that prevent us from moving forward. And then let us do as Mary did: let us look around and look for someone to whom we can be of help! Is there an elderly person I know to whom I can give a little help, company? Everyone, think about it. Or offering a service to someone, a kindness, a phone call? But who can I help? I get up and I help. By helping others, we help ourselves rise up again from difficulties.

The second movement is to *go in haste*. This does not mean to proceed with agitation, in a hurried manner; no, it does not mean this. Instead, it means conducting our days with a joyful step, looking ahead with confidence, without dragging our feet, as slaves to complaints—these complaints ruin so many lives, because one starts complaining and complaining, and life drains away. Complaining leads you always to look for someone to blame. On her way to Elizabeth's house, Mary proceeds with the quick step of one whose heart and life are full of God, full of his joy. So, let us ask ourselves: how is my "step"? Am I proactive or do I linger in melancholy, in sadness? Do I move forward with hope or do I stop and feel sorry for myself? If we proceed with the tired step of grumbling and small talk, we will not bring God to anyone, we will only bring bitterness and dark things. Instead, it is very good for us to cultivate a healthy sense of humor, as for example, Saint Thomas More or Saint Philip Neri did. We can also ask for this grace, the grace of a healthy sense of humor: it does so much good. Let us not forget that the first act of charity we can do for our neighbors is to offer them a serene and smiling face. It is bringing the joy of Jesus to them, as Mary did with Elizabeth.

Joseph

When Joseph woke up, he did what the angel of the Lord had commanded him and took Mary home as his wife. But he did not consummate their marriage until she gave birth to a son. And he gave him the name Jesus.

—Matthew 1:24-25

Joseph Hears the Voice of the Lord

The Gospel tells us about the events preceding the birth of Jesus, and the Evangelist Matthew presents them from the point of view of St. Joseph, the betrothed of the Virgin Mary.

Joseph and Mary were dwelling in Nazareth; they were not yet living together, because they were not yet married. In the meantime, Mary, after having welcomed the angel's announcement, came to be with child by the power of the Holy Spirit. When Joseph realized this, he was bewildered. The Gospel does not explain what his thoughts were, but it does tell us the essential: he seeks to do the will of God and is ready for the most radical renunciation. Rather than defending himself and asserting his rights, Joseph chooses what for him is an enormous sacrifice. And the Gospel tells us: "Joseph, being a just man and unwilling to put her to shame, resolved to send her away quietly" (1:19).

This brief sentence reveals a true inner drama if we think about the love that Joseph had for Mary! But even in these circumstances, Joseph intends to do the will of God and decides, surely with great sorrow, to send Mary away quietly. We need to meditate on these words in order to understand the great trial that Joseph had to endure in the days preceding Jesus' birth. It was a trial similar to the sacrifice of Abraham, when God asked him for his son Isaac (cf. Gen 22): to give up what was most precious, the person most beloved.

But as in the case of Abraham, the Lord intervenes: he found the faith he was looking for and he opens up a different path, a path of love and of happiness. "Joseph," he says, "do not fear to take Mary your wife, for that which is conceived in her is of the Holy Spirit" (Mt 1:20).

This Gospel passage reveals to us the greatness of St. Joseph's heart and soul. He was following a good plan for his life, but God was reserving another plan for him, a greater mission. Joseph was a man who always listened to the voice of God, he was deeply sensitive to his secret will, he was a man attentive to the messages that came to him from the depths of his heart and from on high. He did not persist in following his own plan for his life, he did not allow bitterness to poison his soul; rather, he was ready to make himself available to the news that, in such a bewildering way, was being presented to him. And thus, he was a good man. He did not hate, and he did not allow bitterness to poison his soul. Yet how many times does hatred, or even dislike and bitterness poison our souls! And this is harmful. Never allow it: he is an example of this. And Joseph thereby became even freer and greater. By accepting himself according to God's design, Joseph fully finds himself, beyond himself. His freedom to renounce even what is his, the possession of his very life, and his full interior availability to the will of God, challenges us and shows us the way.

Let us make ourselves ready to celebrate Christmas by contemplating Mary and Joseph: Mary, the woman full of grace who had the courage to entrust herself totally to the Word of God; Joseph, the faithful and just man who chose to believe the Lord rather than listen to the voices of doubt and human pride. With them, let us walk together toward Bethlehem.

Let's Welcome Surprises, Just Like Joseph

What does Joseph say to us today? We too have our dreams, and perhaps we think of them more; we talk about them together at Christmas. Perhaps we long for some dreams that were shattered and we see that our best expectations have to come face to face with the unexpected, disconcerting situations. And when this happens, Joseph shows us the way. We should not give in to negative feelings, like anger or isolation—this is the wrong way! Instead, we must attentively welcome surprises, life's surprises, even the crises. When we find ourselves in crisis, we should not make decisions quickly and instinctively, but rather sift through them like Joseph did, who "considered everything" (cf. v. 20), and base ourselves on the underlying criterium: God's mercy. When one experiences a crisis without giving in to isolation, anger, and fear, but keeps the door open to God, He can intervene. He is an expert in transforming crises into dreams—yes, *God opens crises into new horizons* we never would have imagined before, perhaps not as we would expect, but in the way he knows how. And these, brothers and sisters, are God's horizons—surprising—but infinitely broader and more beautiful than ours! May the Virgin Mary help us live open to God's surprises.

The Keeper of Jesus

At Mary's side, shown protecting the Child and his Mother, stands Saint Joseph. He is usually depicted with staff in hand, or holding up a lamp. Saint Joseph plays an important role in the life of Jesus and Mary. He is the guardian who tirelessly protects his family. When God warned him of Herod's threat, he did not hesitate to set out and flee to Egypt (cf. Mt 2:13-15). And once the danger had passed, he brought the family back to Nazareth, where he was to be the first teacher of Jesus as a boy and then as a young man. Joseph treasured in his heart the great mystery surrounding Jesus and Mary his spouse; as a just man, he entrusted himself always to God's will, and put it into practice.

This Was a Model Educator

St. Joseph is deserving of all our gratitude and devotion for the way in which he guarded over the Holy Virgin and her Son Jesus. Being a guardian is the distinctive trait of Joseph: Being the guardian is his great mission.

Today I would like to take up the theme of guardianship under a particular aspect: the *educational* aspect. We look to Joseph as the model educator, who *watches over and accompanies* Jesus as he grows "in wisdom, age and grace," as the Gospel says. He was not Jesus' father: the father of Jesus was God, but he was a father to Jesus, he was a father to Jesus in order to help him grow. And how did he help him grow? In wisdom, age and grace.

Let us begin with *age*, which is the most natural dimension, physical and psychological growth. Joseph together with Mary, cared for Jesus above all from this point of view, that is he "raised" him, taking care that he lacked nothing he needed for healthy development. Let us not forget that guarding faithfully over the Child's life also entailed the Flight to Egypt, the harsh experience of living as refugees—Joseph was a refugee with Mary and Jesus—so as to escape the threat of Herod. Then, once they had returned home and were settled in Nazareth, there was a long period in Jesus' life spent with his family. In those years Joseph instructed Jesus in his work, and Jesus learned to be a carpenter with his father Joseph. Thus Joseph raised Jesus.

Let us move to the second dimension of his education: "*wisdom*." Joseph was for Jesus the example and the teacher of the wisdom that is nourished by the Word of God. We could ponder how Joseph formed the little Jesus to listen to the Sacred Scriptures, above all by accompanying him on Saturday to the Synagogue in Nazareth. Joseph accompanied Jesus so that he would listen to the Word of God in the Synagogue.

And lastly, the dimension of "*grace*." St. Luke always says of Jesus: "the favor of God was upon him" (2:40). Here, of course, the role reserved to St. Joseph is more limited than it was in the area of age and wisdom. But it would be a grave error to think that a father and mother can do nothing to form their child to grow in the grace of God. To grow in age, to grow in wisdom, and to grow in grace: this is the work Joseph did with Jesus to help him grow in these three ways, to aid his growth.

With a Father's Heart

With a Father's heart: that is how Joseph loved Jesus, whom all four Gospels refer to as *"the son of Joseph."*

Matthew and Luke, the two Evangelists who speak most of Joseph, tell us very little, yet enough for us to appreciate what sort of father he was and the mission entrusted to him by God's providence.

We know that Joseph was a lowly carpenter (cf. Mt 13:55), betrothed to Mary (cf. Mt 1:18; Lk 1:27). He was a "just man" (Mt 1:19), ever ready to carry out God's will as revealed to him in the Law (cf. Lk 2:22,27,39) and through four dreams (cf. Mt 1:20; 2:13,19,22). After a long and tiring journey from Nazareth to Bethlehem, he beheld the birth of the Messiah in a stable, since "there was no place for them" elsewhere (cf. Lk 2:7). He witnessed the adoration of the shepherds (cf. Lk 2:8-20) and the Magi (cf. Mt 2:1-12), who represented respectively the people of Israel and the pagan peoples.

Joseph had the courage to become the legal father of Jesus, to whom he gave the name revealed by the angel: "You shall call his name Jesus, for he will save his people from their sins" (Mt 1:21). As we know, for ancient peoples, to give a name to a person or to a thing, as Adam did in the account in the Book of Genesis (cf. 2:19-20), was to establish a relationship.

In the Temple, forty days after Jesus' birth, Joseph and Mary offered their child to the Lord and listened with amazement to Simeon's prophecy concerning Jesus and his Mother (cf. Lk 2:22-35). To protect Jesus from Herod, Joseph dwelt as a foreigner in Egypt (cf. Mt 2:13-18). After returning to his own country, he led a hidden life in the tiny and obscure village of Nazareth in Galilee, far from Bethlehem, his ancestral town, and from Jerusalem and the Temple. Of Nazareth it was said, "No prophet is to rise" (cf. Jn 7:52) and indeed, "Can anything good come out of Nazareth?" (cf. Jn 1:46). When, during a pilgrimage to Jerusalem, Joseph and Mary lost track of the twelve-year-old Jesus, they anxiously sought him out and they found him in the Temple, in discussion with the doctors of the Law (cf. Lk 2:41-50).

After Mary, the Mother of God, no saint is mentioned more frequently in the papal magisterium than Joseph, her spouse. My Predecessors reflected on the message contained in the limited information handed down by the Gospels in order to appreciate more fully his central role in the history of salvation. Blessed Pius IX declared him "Patron of the Catholic Church," Venerable Pius XII proposed him as "Patron of Workers," and Saint John Paul II as "Guardian of the Redeemer." Saint Joseph is universally invoked as the "patron of a happy death"....

Each of us can discover in Joseph—the man who goes unnoticed, a daily, discreet and hidden presence—an intercessor, a support and a guide in times of trouble. Saint Joseph reminds us that those who appear hidden or in the shadows can play an incomparable role in the history of salvation. A word of recognition and of gratitude is due to them all.

Bethlehem

Jesus was born in Bethlehem in Judea,
during the time of King Herod.

—Matthew 2:1

The Taste of Bread

Bethlehem: the name means *house of bread*. In this "house," the
Lord today wants to encounter all mankind. He knows that
we need food to live. Yet he also knows that the nourishments
of this world do not satisfy the heart....

In Bethlehem, we discover that the life of God can enter
into our hearts and dwell there. If we welcome that gift, history
changes, starting with each of us. For once Jesus dwells in our
heart, the center of life is no longer my ravenous and selfish ego,
but the One who is born and lives for love. Tonight, as we hear
the summons to go up to Bethlehem, the house of bread, let us ask
ourselves: What is the bread of my life, what is it that I cannot do
without? Is it the Lord, or something else? Then, as we enter the
stable, sensing in the tender poverty of the newborn Child a new
fragrance of life, the scent of simplicity, let us ask ourselves: Do I
really need all these material objects and complicated recipes for
living? Can I manage without all these unnecessary extras and live
a life of greater simplicity? In Bethlehem, beside where Jesus lay,
we see people who themselves had made a journey: Mary, Joseph,
and the shepherds. Jesus is bread for the journey. He does not like
long, drawn-out meals, but bids us rise quickly from the table in

order to serve, like bread broken for others. Let us ask ourselves: At Christmas do I break my bread with those who have none?...

"Let us go now to Bethlehem" (Lk 2:15). With these words, the shepherds set out. We too, Lord, want to go up to Bethlehem. Today too, the road is uphill: the heights of our selfishness need to be surmounted, and we must not lose our footing or slide into worldliness and consumerism.

I want to come to Bethlehem, Lord, because there you await me. I want to realize that you, lying in a manger, are *the bread of my life.* I need the tender fragrance of your love so that I, in turn, can be bread broken for the world. Take me upon your shoulders, Good Shepherd; loved by you, I will be able to love my brothers and sisters and to take them by the hand. Then it will be Christmas, when I can say to you: "Lord you know everything; you know that I love you" (cf. Jn 21:17).

Bethlehem, Land of Humility

We note the place in which Jesus was born: *Bethlehem.* A small village in Judea where, thousands of years earlier, David was born, the shepherd boy chosen by God to be the King of Israel. Bethlehem is not a capital city, and for this reason is preferred by divine Providence, who loves to act through the little ones and the humble. In that birthplace was born the highly anticipated "Son of David," Jesus, in whom the hope of God and the hope of man meet.

From Bethlehem a Spark of Hope

The Son of God had to be born in a stable because his own had no room for him. "He came to what was his own and his own people did not accept him" (Jn 1:11). And there, amid the gloom of a city that had no room or place for the stranger from afar, amid the darkness of a bustling city which in this case seemed to want to build itself up by turning its back on others… it was precisely there that the revolutionary spark of God's love was kindled. In Bethlehem, a small chink opens up for those who have lost their land, their country, their dreams; even for those overcome by the asphyxia produced by a life of isolation.

Let's Go Back to Bethlehem

As we take one last look at the crib, in the distance we glimpse the *Magi* journeying to worship the Lord. As we look more closely, we see that all around Jesus everything comes together: not only do we see the poor, the shepherds, but also the learned and the rich, the Magi. In Bethlehem, rich and poor come together, those who worship, like the Magi, and those who work, like the shepherds. Everything is unified when Jesus is at the center: not our ideas about Jesus, but Jesus himself, the living One.

So then, dear brothers and sisters, *let us return to Bethlehem*, let us return to the origins: to the essentials of faith, to our first love, to adoration and charity. Let us look at the Magi who make their pilgrim way, and as a synodal Church, a journeying Church, let us go to Bethlehem, where God is in man and man in God. There the Lord takes first place and is worshipped; there the poor have the place nearest him; there the shepherds and Magi are joined in a fraternity beyond all labels and classifications. May God enable us to be a worshipping, poor and fraternal Church. That is what is essential. Let us go back to Bethlehem.

The Stable

This will be a sign to you:
You will find a baby wrapped in cloths
and lying in a manger.

—Luke 2:12

Hay Is the Cradle of Jesus

The origin of the Christmas crèche is found in certain details of Jesus' birth in Bethlehem, as related in the Gospels. The evangelist Luke says simply that Mary "gave birth to her first-born son and wrapped him in swaddling cloths, and laid him in a manger, because there was no place for them in the inn" (2:7). Because Jesus was laid in a manger, the Nativity scene is known in Italian as a *presepe*, from the Latin word *praesepium*, meaning "manger."

Coming into this world, the Son of God was laid in the place where animals feed. Hay became the first bed of the One who would reveal himself as "the bread come down from heaven" (Jn 6:41). Saint Augustine, with other Church Fathers, was impressed by this symbolism: "Laid in a manger, he became our food" (*Sermon* 189, 4). Indeed, the Nativity scene evokes a number of the mysteries of Jesus' life and brings them close to our own daily lives.

The Manger Teaches Us a Lot

Bethlehem is the turning point that alters the course of history. There, in the *house of bread*, God is born in a *manger*. It is as if he wanted to say: "Here I am, as your food." He does not take, but gives us to eat; he does not give us a mere thing, but his very self. In Bethlehem, we discover that God does not take life, but gives it. To us, who from birth are used to taking and eating, Jesus begins to say: "Take and eat. This is my body" (Mt 26:26). The tiny body of the Child of Bethlehem speaks to us of a new way to live our lives: not by devouring and hoarding, but by sharing and giving. God makes himself small so that he can be our food. By feeding on him, the bread of life, we can *be reborn in love*, and break the spiral of grasping and greed. From the "house of bread," Jesus brings us back home, so that we can become God's family, brothers and sisters to our neighbors. Standing before the manger, we understand that the food of life is not material riches but love, not gluttony but charity, not ostentation but simplicity.

The Lord knows that we need to be fed daily. That is why he offered himself to us every day of his life: from the manger in Bethlehem to the Upper Room in Jerusalem. Today too, on the altar, he becomes bread broken for us; he knocks at our door, to enter and eat with us (cf. Rev 3:20). At Christmas, we on earth receive Jesus, the bread from heaven. It is a bread that never grows stale, but enables us even now to have a foretaste of eternal life.

A Stable Was the House of the Lord

"The poor cannot wait." It is beautiful! And this makes me think of Jesus born in a stable; he was not born in a home. Afterwards he had to flee, to go to Egypt to save his life. Then he returned to his home in Nazareth. And I think, also in reading what is written there, of the many families who do not have a home, either because they never had one or because they lost it for any number of reasons. Family and home go together. It is very difficult to bring up a family without living in a house. This Christmastide, I invite everyone—persons, social institutions, authorities—to do everything possible so that every family might have a home.

Joseph and Mary Impersonate the Homeless

So many other footsteps are hidden in the footsteps of Joseph and Mary. We see the tracks of entire families forced to set out in our own day. We see the tracks of millions of persons who do not choose to go away but, driven from their land, leave behind their dear ones. In many cases this departure is filled with hope, hope for the future; yet for many others this departure can only have one name: survival. Surviving the Herods of today, who, to impose their power and increase their wealth, see no problem in shedding innocent blood.

Mary and Joseph, for whom there was no room, are the first to embrace the One who comes to give all of us our document of citizenship. The One who in his poverty and humility proclaims and shows that true power and authentic freedom are shown in honoring and assisting the weak and the frail.

The Manger of Rejection and Indifference

The Gospel reveals a paradox. It speaks of the emperor, the governor, the high and mighty of those times, yet God does not make himself present there. He appears not in the splendor of a royal palace, but in the poverty of a stable; not in pomp and show, but in simplicity of life; not in power, but in astonishing smallness. In order to meet him, we need to go where he is. We need to bow down, to humble ourselves, to make ourselves small. The newborn Child challenges us. He calls us to leave behind fleeting illusions and to turn to what is essential, to renounce our insatiable cravings, to abandon our endless yearning for things we will never have. We do well to leave such things behind, in order to discover, in the simplicity of the divine Child, peace, joy and the luminous meaning of life.

Let us allow the Child in the manger to challenge us, but let us also be challenged by all those children in today's world who are lying not in a crib, caressed with affection by their mothers and fathers, but in squalid "mangers that devour dignity." Children who hide underground to escape bombardment, on the pavements of large cities, in the hold of a boat overladen with immigrants… Let us allow ourselves to be challenged by those children who are not allowed to be born, by those who cry because no one relieves their hunger, by those who hold in their hands not toys, but weapons.

The mystery of Christmas, which is light and joy, challenges and unsettles us because it is at once a *mystery of hope and of sadness*. It has a *taste of sadness*, inasmuch as love is not accepted, and life discarded. Such was the case with Joseph and Mary, who met with closed doors, and placed Jesus in a manger, "because there was no place for them in the inn" (v. 7). Jesus was born rejected by some and regarded by many others with indifference. Today too, that same indifference can exist, whenever Christmas becomes a holiday with ourselves at the center rather than Jesus; when the lights of shop windows push the light of God into the shadows; when we are enthused about gifts but indifferent to our neighbors in need. This worldliness has kidnapped Christmas; we need to liberate it!

Yet Christmas has above all a *taste of hope* because, for all the darkness in our lives, God's light shines forth. His gentle light does not frighten us. God, who is in love with us, draws us to himself with his tenderness, by being born poor and frail in our midst, as one of us. He is born in Bethlehem, which means "house of bread." In this way, he seems to tell us that he is born as *bread for us*; he enters our life to give us his life; he comes into our world to give us his love. He does not come to devour or to lord it over us, but instead to feed and serve us. There is a straight line between the manger and the cross where Jesus will become *bread that is broken*. It is the straight line of love that gives and saves, the love that brings light to our lives and peace to our hearts.

The Angels

Suddenly a great company of the heavenly host
appeared with the angel, praising God and saying,

'Glory to God in the highest heaven,
and on earth peace to those on whom his
favor rests.'

—Luke 2:13-14

The Angels Know Who They Rejoice Over

The very *choir of angels* proclaims from on high the great design that the Child fulfills: "Glory to God in the highest heaven, and on earth peace to those on whom his favor rests" (2:14). Christian hope is expressed in praise and gratitude to God, who has initiated his Kingdom of love, justice, and peace.

In these days, contemplating the Nativity scene, we prepare ourselves for the Birth of the Lord. It will truly be a celebration if we welcome Jesus, the seed of hope that God sets down in the furrows of our individual and community history.

Let's Celebrate the One Who Is Born

In the Nativity scene we see the love of a mother who embraces her newborn child, the love of a father who protects and defends his family, we see pastors who are moved by the sight of the newborn, angels who celebrate the coming of the Lord…

The Shepherds

And there were shepherds living out in the fields nearby, keeping watch over their flocks at night. An angel of the Lord appeared to them, and the glory of the Lord shone around them.

—Luke 2:8-9

The First to See Jesus

The first people to see the humble glory of the Savior, after Mary and Joseph, were the shepherds of Bethlehem. They recognized the sign proclaimed to them by the angels and adored the Child. Those humble and watchful men are an example for believers of every age who, before the mystery of Jesus, are not scandalized by his poverty. Rather, like Mary, they trust in God's word and contemplate his glory with simple eyes. Before the mystery of the Word made flesh, Christians in every place confess with the words of the Evangelist John: "We have beheld his glory, glory as of the only-begotten Son from the Father, full of grace and truth" (Jn 1:14).

God Is Born and Embraces the Excluded

That night, the One who had no place to be born is proclaimed to those who had no place at the table or in the streets of the city. The shepherds are the first to hear this Good News. By reason of their work, they were men and women forced to live on the edges of society. Their state of life, and the places they had to stay, prevented them from observing all the ritual prescriptions of religious purification; as a result, they were considered unclean. Their skin, their clothing, their smell, their way of speaking, their origin, all betrayed them. Everything about them generated mistrust. They were men and women to be kept at a distance, to be feared. They were considered pagans among the believers, sinners among the just, foreigners among the citizens. Yet to them—pagans, sinners, and foreigners—the angel says: "Do not be afraid; for see—I am bringing you good news of great joy for the people: to you is born this day in the city of David a Savior, who is the Messiah, the Lord" (Lk 2:10-11).

This is the joy that we tonight are called to share, to celebrate, and to proclaim. The joy with which God, in his infinite mercy, has embraced us *pagans, sinners, and foreigners*, and demands that we do the same.

We too, Traveling Like Them

"Let us go over to Bethlehem and see this thing that has happened, which the Lord has made known to us" (Lk 2:15). So the shepherds tell one another after the proclamation of the angels. A beautiful lesson emerges from these simple words. Unlike so many other people, busy with many things, the shepherds become the first to see the most essential thing of all: the gift of salvation. It is the humble and the poor who greet the event of the Incarnation. The shepherds respond to God who comes to meet us in the Infant Jesus by setting out to meet him with love, gratitude, and awe. Thanks to Jesus, this encounter between God and his children gives birth to our religion and accounts for its unique beauty, so wonderfully evident in the Nativity scene.

Watch in the Night

The shepherds of Bethlehem also tell us how to go forth to meet the Lord. They were keeping watch by night: they were not sleeping, but doing what Jesus often asks all of us to do, namely, *be watchful* (cf. Mt 25:13; Mk 13:35; Lk 21:36). They remain alert and attentive in the darkness; and God's light then "shone around them" (Lk 2:9). This is also the case for us. Our life can be marked by *waiting*, which amid the gloom of our problems hopes in the Lord and yearns for his coming; then we will receive his life. Or our life can be marked by *wanting*, where all that matters are our own strengths and abilities; our heart then remains barred to God's light. The Lord loves to be awaited, and we cannot await him lying on a couch, sleeping. So the shepherds immediately set out: we are told that they "went with haste" (v. 16). They do not just stand there like those who think they have already arrived and need do nothing more. Instead they set out; they leave their flocks unguarded; they take a risk for God. And after seeing Jesus, although they were not men of fine words, they go off to proclaim his birth, so that "all who heard were amazed at what the shepherds told them" (v. 18).

To keep watch, to set out, to risk, to recount the beauty: all these are *acts of love*. The Good Shepherd, who at Christmas comes to give his life to the sheep, will later, at Easter, ask Peter, and through him all of us, the ultimate question: "Do you love me?" (Jn 21:15). The future of the flock will depend on how that question is answered. Tonight we too are asked to respond to Jesus with the words: "I love you." The answer given by each is essential for the whole flock.

Raising Our Eyes to Heaven

On Christmas Eve Jesus manifested himself to shepherds, humble and scorned men—some say brigands. They were the first to bring a little warmth to that gelid cave in Bethlehem. Then the Magi arrived from faraway lands. They too were mysteriously drawn by that Child. The shepherds and the Wise Men were very different from each other; however, they had one thing in common: heaven. The shepherds of Bethlehem immediately hastened to see Jesus, not because they were particularly good, but because they kept watch in the night and, raising their eyes to heaven, they saw a sign, they heard its message and followed it. It was the same for the Magi: they observed the heavens, saw a new star, interpreted the sign, and set out on their journey from afar. The shepherds and the Wise Men teach us that in order to encounter Jesus it is necessary to be able to lift our gaze to heaven, not to withdraw into ourselves, into our own selfishness, but to have our heart and mind open to the horizons of God, who always surprises us, to be able to welcome his messages and respond with readiness and generosity.

We Enter Christmas with the Shepherds

It is a *night of light*. The light prophesied by Isaiah (cf. 9:1), which was to shine on those who walked in a land of darkness, has appeared and enveloped the shepherds of Bethlehem (cf. Lk 2:9).

The shepherds discover simply that "a child has been born to us" (Is 9:5). They realize that all this glory, all this joy, all this light, converges to a single point, the *sign* that the angel indicated to them: "You will find a child wrapped in swaddling clothes and lying in a manger" (Lk 2:12). This is *the enduring sign* for all who would find Jesus. Not just then, but also today. If we want to celebrate Christmas authentically, we need to contemplate this sign: the frail simplicity of a tiny newborn child, the meekness with which he is placed in a manger, the tender affection with which he is wrapped in his swaddling clothes. That is where God is....

Jesus is the straight line of love that gives and saves, the love that brings light to our lives and peace to our hearts. That night, the shepherds understood this. They were among the marginalized of those times. Yet no one is marginalized in the sight of God, and that Christmas, they themselves were the guests. People who felt sure of themselves, self-sufficient, were at home with their possessions. It was the shepherds who "set out with haste" (cf. Lk 2:16). Tonight, may we too be challenged and called by Jesus. Let us approach him with trust, starting from all those things that make us feel marginalized, from our limitations and our sins. Let us be touched by the tenderness that saves. Let us draw close to God who draws close to us. Let us pause to gaze upon the crib, and relive in our imagination the birth of Jesus: light and peace, dire poverty and rejection. With the shepherds, let us enter into the real Christmas, bringing to Jesus all that we are, our alienation, our unhealed wounds, our sins. Then, in Jesus, we will enjoy the taste of the true spirit of Christmas: the beauty of being loved by God. With Mary and Joseph, let us pause before the manger, before Jesus who is born as bread for my life. Contemplating his humble and infinite love, let us simply tell him: Thank you. Thank you because you have done all this *for me*.

The Most Precious Gift

A charming legend relates that at the birth of Jesus the shepherds hurried to the stable with different gifts. Each brought what he had; some brought the fruits of their labor, others some precious item. But as they were all presenting their gifts, there was one shepherd who had nothing to give. He was extremely poor; he had no gift to present. As the others were competing to offer their gifts, he stood apart, embarrassed. At a certain point, Saint Joseph and Our Lady found it hard to receive all those gifts, especially Mary, who had to hold the baby. Seeing that shepherd with empty hands, she asked him to draw near. And she put the baby Jesus in his arms. That shepherd, in accepting him, became aware of having received what he did not deserve, of holding in his arms the greatest gift of all time. He looked at his hands, those hands that seemed to him always empty; they had become the cradle of God. He felt himself loved and, overcoming his embarrassment, began to show Jesus to the others, for he could not keep for himself the gift of gifts.

Dear brother, dear sister, if your hands seem empty, if you think your heart is poor in love, this night is for you. *The grace of God has appeared* to shine forth in your life. Accept it and the light of Christmas will shine forth in you.

The Light

Arise, shine, for your light has come,
and the glory of the Lord rises upon you.
See, darkness covers the earth
and thick darkness is over the peoples,
but the Lord rises upon you
and his glory appears over you.

—Isaiah 60:1-2

On Christmas Night, a Great Light Shines

"The people who walked in darkness have seen a great light; those who dwelt in a land of deep darkness, on them has light shined" (Is 9:1). "An angel of the Lord appeared to [the shepherds] and the glory of the Lord shone around them" (Lk 2:9). This is how the liturgy of this holy Christmas night presents to us the birth of the Savior: as the light which pierces and dispels the deepest darkness. The presence of the Lord in the midst of his people cancels the sorrow of defeat and the misery of slavery, and ushers in joy and happiness.

We too, in this blessed night, have come to the house of God. We have passed through the darkness which envelops the earth, guided by the flame of faith which illuminates our steps, and enlivened by the hope of finding the "great light." By opening our hearts, we also can contemplate the miracle of that child-sun who, arising from on high, illuminates the horizon.

Our Life Is Enlightened

Tonight "a great light" shines forth (Is 9:1); the light of Jesus' birth shines all about us. How true and timely are the words of the prophet Isaiah which we have just heard: "You have brought abundant joy and great rejoicing" (9:2)! Our heart was already joyful in awaiting this moment; now that joy abounds and over-flows, for the promise has been at last fulfilled….

Today, the Son of God is born, and everything changes…. The true light has come to illumine our lives so often beset by the darkness of sin. Today we once more discover who we are! Tonight we have been shown the way to reach the journey's end. Now must we put away all fear and dread, for the light shows us the path to Bethlehem. We must not be laggards; we are not permitted to stand idle. We must set out to see our Savior lying in a manger.

Light Is the Love of God

"Those who dwelt in a land of deep darkness, on them has light shined" (Is 9:1). The prophecy we heard in the first reading was fulfilled in the Gospel: as shepherds kept watch over their flocks by night, "the glory of the Lord shone around them" (Lk 2:9). In the midst of our earthly night, a light appeared from heaven. What is the meaning of this light that shone in the darkness? Saint Paul tells us: "The grace of God has appeared." The grace of God, "bringing salvation to all" (Tit 2:11), has shone on our world this night.

But what is this grace? It is divine love, the love that changes lives, renews history, liberates from evil, fills hearts with peace and joy. Tonight the love of God has been revealed to us: it is Jesus.

Jesus Can Make Every Darkness Shine

Isaiah's vision (cf. 60:1-6), resounds in our time and is more timely than ever: "darkness covers the earth, and thick darkness the peoples" (cf. v. 2). With this background, the prophet announces the light: the light given by God to Jerusalem and destined to illuminate the path of all the peoples. This light has the power to attract everyone, near and far; everyone sets out on the path to reach it (cf. v. 3). It is a vision that opens the heart, that makes it easier to breathe, that invites hope. Certainly, darkness is present and threatening in everyone's life and in the history of humanity, but God's light is more powerful. It is a matter of welcoming it so that it might shine on everyone. But we can ask ourselves: where is this light? The prophet glimpsed it from afar, but that was already enough to fill the heart of Jerusalem with irrepressible joy.

Where is this light? The Evangelist Matthew, in his turn, recounting the episode of the Magi (cf. 2:1-12), shows that this light is the Babe of Bethlehem; it is Jesus, even if his kingship was not accepted by everyone. Rather some rejected it, like Herod. He is the star who appeared on the horizon, the awaited Messiah, the One through whom God would establish his kingdom of love, his kingdom of justice, his kingdom of peace. He was born not only for some, but for all men and women, for all peoples. The light is for all peoples, salvation is for all peoples.

And how does this "irradiation" happen? How does Christ's light shine in every place and at all times? It has its own method of disseminating. It does not do so through the powerful means of this world's empires which always seek to seize power. No, the light of Christ spreads through the proclamation of the Gospel. Proclamation, word, and witness. And with this same "method" chosen by God to come among us: incarnation, that is, by drawing near to the other, encountering the other, assuming the reality of the other, and bringing the witness of our faith, each one. This is the only way that the light of Christ, who is Love, can shine in those who welcome it and attract others. Christ's light does not expand only through words, through phony, commercial methods... No, no. Faith, word, and witness: this is how the light of Christ expands. The star is Christ, but we too can and must be the star for our brothers and our sisters, as witnesses of the treasures of goodness and of infinite mercy which the Redeemer offers freely to everyone. The light of Christ does not expand through proselytism. It expands through witness, through the confession of the faith. Also through martyrdom.

Therefore, the condition is to welcome this light within, to welcome it ever increasingly. Woe if we think we possess it; woe if we think we only need to "manage" it! Like the Magi, we too are called to allow ourselves to be fascinated, attracted, guided, illuminated, and converted by Christ: it is the journey of faith, through prayer and the contemplation of the works of God, which continually fill us with joy and wonder, an ever-new wonder. That wonder is always the first step to go forward in this light.

Evil Doers Hate Light

St. John says in the Gospel that we read today: "In him was life, and the life was the light of men. The light shines in the darkness, and the darkness has not overcome it.... The true light that enlightens every man was coming into the world" (1:4-5, 9). Men speak much of light, but they often prefer the deceptive tranquility of darkness. We speak a lot about peace, but we often turn to war or choose the complicity of silence, or do nothing concrete to build peace. In fact, St. John says that "He came to his own home, and his own people received him not" (Jn 1:11); for "this is the judgment, that the light—Jesus—has come into the world, and men loved darkness rather than light, because their deeds were evil. For everyone who does evil hates the light, and does not come to the light, lest his deeds should be exposed" (Jn 3:19-20). This is what St. John says in the Gospel. The heart of man may reject the light and prefer the shadows, because light lays bare his evil deeds. Those who do evil hate light. Those who do evil hate peace.

The Magi

When they saw the star, they were overjoyed. On coming to the house, they saw the child with his mother Mary, and they bowed down and worshipped him. Then they opened their treasures and presented him with gifts of gold, frankincense and myrrh.

—Matthew 2:10-11

Men Searching

According to tradition, the wise men were sages, watchers of the constellations, observers of the heavens, in a cultural and religious context which saw the stars as having significance and power over human affairs. The wise men represent men and women *who seek God in the world's religions and philosophies*: an unending quest. Men and women who seek God.

The wise men point out to us the path of our journey through life. They sought the true Light. As a liturgical hymn of Epiphany which speaks of their experience puts it: *"Lumen requirunt lumine"*; by following *a* light, they sought *the* light, *"Lumen requirunt lumine."* They set out in search of God. Having seen the sign of the star, they grasped its message and set off on a long journey.

It is *the Holy Spirit* who called them and prompted them to set out; during their journey they were also to have a *personal encounter* with the true God.

Along the way, the wise men encountered *many difficulties*. Once they reached Jerusalem, they went to the palace of the king, for they thought it obvious that the new king would be born in the royal palace. There they lost sight of the star. How often sight of the star is lost! And, having lost sight of the star, they met with *a temptation*, placed there by the devil: it was the deception of Herod. King Herod was interested in the child, not to worship him but to eliminate him. Herod is the powerful man who sees others only as rivals. Deep down, he also considers God a rival, indeed the most dangerous rival of all. In the palace the wise men experience a moment of obscurity, of desolation, which they manage to overcome thanks to the prompting of the Holy Spirit, who speaks through the prophecies of sacred Scripture. These indicate that the Messiah is to be born in Bethlehem, the city of David.

At that point they resume their journey, and once more they see the star; the evangelist says that they "rejoiced exceedingly" (Mt 2:10). Coming to Bethlehem, they found "the child with Mary his mother" (Mt 2:11). After that of Jerusalem, this was their *second great temptation*: to reject this smallness. But instead, "they fell down and worshiped him," offering him their precious symbolic gifts. Again, it is *the grace of the Holy Spirit* which assists them. That grace, which through the star had called them and led them along the way, now *lets them enter into the mystery*. The star which led them on the journey allows them to enter into the mystery. Led by the Spirit, they come to realize that God's criteria are quite different from those of men, that God does not manifest himself in the power of this world, but speaks to us in the humbleness of his love. God's love is great. God's love is powerful. But the love of God is humble, yes, very humble. The wise men are thus models of conversion to the true faith, since they believed more in the goodness of God than in the apparent splendor of power.

And so we can ask ourselves: what is *the mystery in which God is hidden?* Where can I find him? All around us we see wars, the exploitation of children, torture, trafficking in arms, trafficking in persons… In all these realities, in these, the least of our brothers and sisters who are enduring these difficult situations, there is Jesus (cf. Mt 25:40,45). The crib points us to a different path from the one cherished by the thinking of this world: it is the path of *God's self-abasement*, that humility of God's love by which he abases himself, he completely lowers himself, his glory concealed in the manger of Bethlehem, on the cross upon Calvary, in each of our suffering brothers and sisters.

The wise men *entered into the mystery*. They passed from human calculations to the mystery: this was their conversion. And our own? Let us ask the Lord to let us undergo that same journey of conversion experienced by the wise men. Let us ask him to protect us and to set us free from the temptations which hide the star. To let us always feel the troubling question: "Where is the star?" whenever—amid the deceptions of this world—we lose sight of it. To let us know ever anew God's mystery, and not to be scandalized by the "sign," that sign spoken of by the angels, which points to "a babe wrapped in swaddling cloths, lying in a manger" (Lk 2:12), and to have the humility to ask the Mother, our Mother, to show him to us. To find the courage to be liberated from our illusions, our presumptions, our "lights," and to seek this courage in the humility of faith and in this way to encounter the Light, *Lumen*, like the holy wise men. May we enter into the mystery. So may it be. Amen.

When You Miss God

"Where is the child who has been born king of the Jews? For we have observed his star in the East, and have come to worship him" (Mt 2:2).

With these words, the Magi, come from afar, tell us the reason for their long journey: they came to worship the newborn King.

To see and to worship. These two actions stand out in the Gospel account. We saw a star and we want to worship.

These men *saw a star* that made them set out. The discovery of something unusual in the heavens sparked a whole series of events. The star did not shine just for them, nor did they have special DNA to be able to see it. As one of the Church Fathers rightly noted, the Magi did not set out because they had seen the star, but they saw the star because they had already set out" (cf. Saint John Chrysostom). Their hearts were open to the horizon and they could see what the heavens were showing them, for they were guided by an inner restlessness. They were open to something new.

The Magi thus personify all those who believe, those who long for God, who yearn for their home, their heavenly homeland. They reflect the image of all those who in their lives have not let their hearts be anesthetized.

Those men came from the East to worship, and they came to do so in the place befitting a king: a palace. This is significant. Their quest led them there, for it was fitting that a king should be born in a palace, amid a court and all his subjects. For that is a sign of power, success, a life of achievement. One might well expect a king to be venerated, feared, and adulated. True, but not necessarily loved. For those are worldly categories, the paltry idols to which we pay homage: the cult of power, outward appearances, and superiority. Idols that promise only sorrow, enslavement, fear.

It was there, in that place, that those men, come from afar, would embark upon their longest journey. There they set out boldly on a more arduous and complicated journey. They had to discover that what they sought was not in a palace, but elsewhere, both existentially and geographically. There, in the palace, they did not see the star guiding them to discover a God who wants to be loved. For only under the banner of freedom, not tyranny, is it possible to realize that the gaze of this unknown but desired king does not abase, enslave, or imprison us. To realize that the gaze of God lifts up, forgives, and heals. To realize that God wanted to be born where we least expected, or perhaps desired, in a place where we so often refuse him. To realize that in God's eyes there is always room for those who are wounded, weary, mistreated, abandoned. That his strength and his power are called mercy. For some of us, how far Jerusalem is from Bethlehem!

Restless Hearts That Yearn for God

The Magi travel toward Bethlehem…. What made these men of the East set out on their journey?

They had excellent reasons not to depart. They were wise men and astrologers, famous and wealthy. Having attained sufficient cultural, social and economic security, they could have remained content with what they already knew and possessed. Instead, they let themselves be unsettled by a question and by a sign: "Where is he who has been born king of the Jews? For we have seen his star…" (Mt 2:2). They did not allow their hearts to retreat into the caves of gloom and apathy; they longed to see the light. They were not content to plod through life, but yearned for new and greater horizons. Their eyes were not fixed here below; they were windows open to the heavens. As Benedict XVI said, the Magi were "men with a restless heart… They were filled with expectation, not satisfied with their secure income and their respectable place in society… They were seekers after God" (*Homily*, 6 January 2013)….

Let us look at the steps they took, and draw some lessons from them.

In the first place, they *set out* at the rising of the star. The Magi teach us that we need to set out anew each day, in life as in faith, for faith is not a suit of armor that encases us; instead, it is a fascinating journey, a constant and restless movement, ever in search of God, always discerning our way forward.

Then, in Jerusalem the Magi *ask questions*: they inquire where the Child is to be found. They teach us that we need to question. We need to listen carefully to the questions of our heart and our conscience, for it is there that God often speaks to us. He addresses us more with questions than with answers. We must learn this well: God addresses us more with questions than with answers. Yet let us also be unsettled by the questions of our children, and by the doubts, hopes, and desires of the men and women of our time. We need to entertain questions.

The Magi then *defy* Herod. They teach us that we need a courageous faith, one that is unafraid to challenge the sinister logic of power, and becomes seeds of justice and fraternity in societies where in our day modern Herods continue to sow death and slaughter the poor and innocent, amid general indifference.

Finally, the Magi *return* "by another way" (Mt 2:12). They challenge us to take new paths. Here we see the creativity of the Spirit who always brings out new things. That is also one of the tasks of the Synod we are currently undertaking: to journey together and to listen to one another, so that the Spirit can suggest to us new ways and paths to bring the Gospel to the hearts of those who are distant, indifferent, or without hope, yet continue to seek what the Magi found: "a great joy" (Mt 2:10). We must always move forward.

At the end of the Magi's journey came the climactic moment: once they arrived at their destination, "they fell down and worshiped the Child" (cf. v. 11). *They worshipped.* Let us never forget this: the journey of faith finds renewed strength and fulfilment only when it is made in the presence of God. Only if we recover our "taste" for adoration will our desire be rekindled. Desire leads us to adoration and adoration renews our desire. For our desire for God can only grow when we place ourselves in his presence.

For Jesus alone heals our desires. From what? From the tyranny of needs. Indeed, our hearts grow sickly whenever our desires coincide merely with our needs. God, on the other hand, elevates our desires; he purifies them and heals them of selfishness, opening them to love for him and for our brothers and sisters. This is why we should not neglect adoration, that prayer of silent adoration which is not so common among us. Please let us not forget adoration.

In this way, like the Magi, we will have the daily certainty that even in the darkest nights a star continues to shine. It is the star of the Lord, who comes to care for our frail humanity. Let us set out on the path toward him. Let us not give apathy and resignation the power to drive us into a cheerless and banal existence. Let our restless hearts embrace the restlessness of the Spirit. The world expects from believers a new burst of enthusiasm for the things of heaven. Like the Magi, let us lift up our eyes, listen to the desire lodged in our hearts, and follow the star that God makes shine above us. As restless seekers, let us remain open to God's surprises. Brothers and sisters, let us dream, let us seek and let us adore.

Generous and Open to What Is New

Having come from the East, they represent all the faraway peoples of the traditional Hebrew faith. Yet they allow themselves to be guided by the star and face a long and perilous journey just to arrive at the destination and to know the truth of the Messiah. The Magi were *open* to 'novelty', and history's greatest and most surprising novelty is revealed to them: God made man. The Magi prostrate themselves before Jesus and offer him symbolic gifts: gold, incense, and myrrh, because seeking the Lord entails not only perseverance on the journey but also generosity of heart. And lastly, they returned "to their own country" (v. 12); and the Gospel states that they returned "by another road." . . . They returned "to their own country," bearing within them the mystery of that humble and poor King; we can imagine that they told everyone about the experience they had had: the salvation offered by God in Christ is for *all mankind*, near and far. It is not possible to "take possession" of that Child: he is a gift for all.

Be Filled with Joy

The Magi teach us that people can come to Christ by a very long route. Men of wealth, sages from afar, athirst for the infinite, they set out on the long and perilous journey that would lead them to Bethlehem (cf. Mt 2:1-12). Great joy comes over them in the presence of the Infant King. They are not scandalized by the poor surroundings, but immediately fall to their knees to worship him. Kneeling before him, they understand that the God who with sovereign wisdom guides the course of the stars also guides the course of history, casting down the mighty and raising up the lowly. Upon their return home, they would certainly have told others of this amazing encounter with the Messiah, thus initiating the spread of the Gospel among the nations.

The Three Gestures of the Magi

Three actions of the Magi guide our journey toward the Lord, who today is revealed as light and salvation for all peoples. The Magi *see the star*, they *set out*, and they *bring gifts*.

Seeing the star. This is where it starts. But why, we might ask, did the Magi alone see the star? Perhaps because few people raised their eyes to heaven. We often make do with looking at the ground: it's enough to have our health, a little money and a bit of entertainment. I wonder if we still know how to look up at the sky. Do we know how to dream, to long for God, to expect the newness he brings, or do we let ourselves be swept along by life, like dry branches before the wind? The Magi were not content with just getting by, with keeping afloat. They understood that to truly live, we need a lofty goal and we need to keep looking up….

Setting out, the second thing the Magi do, is essential if we are to find Jesus. His star demands a decision to take up the journey and to advance tirelessly on our way. It demands that we free ourselves from useless burdens and unnecessary extras that only prove a hindrance, and accept unforeseen obstacles along the map of life. Jesus allows himself to be found by those who seek him, but to find him we need to get up and go, not sit around, but take risks, not stand still, but set out. Jesus makes demands: he tells those who seek him to leave behind the armchair of worldly comforts and the reassuring warmth of hearth and home. Following Jesus is not a polite etiquette to be observed, but a journey to be undertaken. God, who set his people free in the exodus and called new peoples to follow his star, grants freedom and joy always and only in the course of a journey. In other words, if we want to find Jesus, we must overcome our fear of taking risks, our self-satisfaction, and our indolent refusal to ask anything more of life. We need to take risks simply to meet a Child. Yet those risks are immensely worth the effort, since in finding that Child, in discovering his tenderness and love, we rediscover ourselves….

Bringing gifts. Having come to Jesus after a long journey, the Magi do as he does: they bring gifts. Jesus is there to give his life; they offer him their own costly gifts: gold, incense, and myrrh. The Gospel becomes real when the journey of life ends in giving. To give *freely*, for the Lord's sake, without expecting anything in return: this is the sure sign that we have found Jesus. For he says: "The gift you have received, give freely as a gift" (Mt 10:8). To do good without counting the cost, even when unasked, even when you gain nothing thereby, even if it is unpleasant. That is what God wants. He, who became small for our sake, asks us to offer something for the least of his brothers and sisters. Who are they? They are those who have nothing to give in return: the needy, the hungry, the stranger, the prisoner, the poor (cf. Mt 25:31-46). We give a gift pleasing to Jesus when we care for a sick person, spend time with a difficult person, help someone for the sake of helping, or forgive someone who has hurt us. These are gifts freely given, and they cannot be lacking in the lives of Christians. Jesus reminds us that if we only love those who love us, we do as the pagans do (cf. Mt 5:46-47). Today let us look at our hands, so often empty of love, and let us try to think of some gift that we can give without expecting anything in return. That will please the Lord. And let us ask him: "Lord, let me rediscover the joy of giving."

Let us imitate the Magi: looking upward, setting out, and freely offering our gifts.

Whoever Adores Jesus Is Transformed by His Love

In the Gospel (Mt 2:1-12), we heard the Magi begin by stating the reason why they have come: "We have seen his star in the East, and have come to worship him" (v. 2). Worship is the end and goal of their journey. Indeed, when they arrived in Bethlehem, "they saw the child with Mary his mother, and they fell down and worshiped him" (v. 11)….

Worship means going to Jesus without a list of petitions, but with one request alone: to abide with him. It is about discovering that joy and peace increase with praise and thanksgiving.

In worship, we allow Jesus to heal and change us. In worship, we make it possible for the Lord to transform us by his love, to kindle light amid our darkness, to grant us strength in weakness and courage amid trials. Worship means concentrating on what is essential: ridding ourselves of useless things and addictions that anesthetize the heart and confound the mind. In worship, we learn to reject what should *not* be worshipped: the god of money, the god of consumerism, the god of pleasure, the god of success, the god of *self*. Worship means bending low before the Most High and to discover in his presence that life's greatness does not consist in having, but in loving. Worship means recognizing that we are all brothers and sisters before the mystery of a love that bridges every distance: it is to encounter goodness at the source; it is to find in the God of closeness the courage to draw near to others. Worship means knowing how to be silent in the presence of the divine Word, and learning to use words that do not wound but console.

Worship is an act of love that changes our lives. It is to do what the Magi did. To bring gold to the Lord and to tell him that nothing is more precious than he is. To offer him incense and to tell him that only in union with him can our lives rise up to heaven. To present him with myrrh, balm for the bruised and wounded, and to promise him that we will aid our marginalized and suffering neighbors, in whom he himself is present. We usually know how to pray—we ask the Lord, we thank him—but the Church must move forward in her prayer of worship; we must grow in worshiping. This is wisdom that we must learn each day. Praying by worshiping: the prayer of worship.

Dear brothers and sisters, today each one of us can ask: "Am I a Christian who worships?" Many Christians pray but they do not worship. Let us ask ourselves this question: Do we find time for worship in our daily schedules, and do we make room for worship in our communities? It is up to us, as a Church, to put into practice the words we prayed in today's Psalm: "All the peoples on earth will worship you, O Lord." In worshiping, we too will discover, like the Magi, the meaning of our journey. And like the Magi, we too will experience "a great joy" (Mt 2:10).

Illustrious But Humble Men

Let us think about these wise, rich, educated, well-known men who prostrate themselves, that is, they bow down on the ground to adore a baby! This seems a contradiction. Such a humble action performed by such illustrious men is surprising. To prostrate oneself before a leader who presented himself with the trappings of power and glory was something normal at that time. And even today this would not be strange. But before the Babe of Bethlehem, it was not simple. It is not easy to adore this God, whose divinity remains hidden and does not appear triumphant. It means welcoming God's greatness that manifests itself in littleness. This is the message. The Magi humbled themselves before the unheard-of logic of God. They welcomed the Lord not the way they had imagined him to be, but as he was, small and poor. Their prostration is the sign of those who place their own ideas aside and make room for God. It takes humility to do this.

The Gospel stresses this: it does not only say that the Magi worshipped; it emphasizes that *they fell down and worshipped*. Let us understand this detail: worship and prostration go together. By performing this gesture, the Magi manifest their humble acceptance of the One who presented himself in humility. And so it is that they are open to worship God. The treasures they open are images of their open hearts: their true wealth does not consist in their fame, their success, but in their humility, in considering themselves *in need of salvation*. This is the example the Magi give us today.

If we always remain at the center of everything with our ideas, and if we presume to have something to boast of before God, we will never fully encounter him, we will never end up worshipping him. If our pretensions, vanity, stubbornness, competitiveness do not fall by the wayside, we may well end up worshipping someone or something in life, but it will not be the Lord! If instead, we abandon our pretense of self-sufficiency, if we make ourselves little inside, we will then rediscover the wonder of worshipping Jesus because *adoration comes from humility of heart*: those who crave winning do not notice the Lord's presence. Jesus passes nearby and is ignored, as happened to many at that time, but not to the Magi….

The Magi began their journey looking at a star, and they found Jesus. They walked a lot. Today, we can take this piece of advice: look at the star and walk. Never stop walking, but do not stop looking at the star. This is the strong advice for today: look at the star and walk, look at the star and walk.

The Encounter with Jesus Puts the Magi Back on the Road

These wise men from distant lands find the one they wished to meet, after seeking him for so long, undoubtedly through exertion and danger. And when they finally reach their destination, they prostrate before the Child, they praise him and offer him their precious gifts. After that, they resume their journey without delay to return to their lands. But that encounter with the Child has changed them.

The encounter with Jesus does not hold back the Magi. Indeed it instills in them a renewed thrust to return to their countries to recount what they had seen and the joy they had felt. There is a demonstration of God's style in this, of his way of manifesting himself in history. The experience of God does not block us, but frees us. It does not imprison us, but rather puts us back on a journey and delivers us to the familiar places of our lives. The places are and will continue to be the same. However, after the encounter with Jesus, we are *no longer the ones we were*. The encounter with Jesus changes us, transforms us. The Evangelist Matthew highlights that the Magi returned "by another way" (v. 12). They were led to change their path after the angel's warning, so as not to run into Herod and his network of power.

Each experience of encounter with Jesus leads us to take a different road because from him comes a good power that heals the heart and separates us from evil.

There is a wise dynamic between continuity and newness: the Magi return "to their own country" but "by another way." This indicates that *we are the ones who must change*, to transform our way of living, albeit in our everyday environment, to modify our criteria of judgment over the reality that surrounds us. Here lies the difference between the true God and treacherous idols such as money, power, success ... between God and those who promise to give you these idols such as clairvoyants, fortune-tellers, sorcerers. The difference is that idols tie us to them, they make us idol-dependent and we take possession of them.

The true God does not hold us back, nor does he allow himself to be held back by us. He opens paths of newness and freedom because he is the Father who is always with us so that we can grow. If you encounter Jesus, if you have a spiritual encounter with Jesus, remember you must always return to the same places but *by another way*, with another style. It is so. It is the Holy Spirit that Jesus gives us that changes our hearts.

The Star

Where is the one who has been born king of the Jews? We saw his star when it rose and have come to worship him.

—Matthew 2:2

A Star among the Stars

How many stars there are in the sky! And yet the Magi followed a new and different star, which for them shone all the more brightly. They had long peered into the great book of the heavens, seeking an answer to their questions—they had restless hearts —, and at long last the light appeared. That star changed them. It made them leave their daily concerns behind and set out immediately on a journey. They listened to a voice deep within, which led them to follow that light. It was the voice of the Holy Spirit, who works in all people. The star guided them, until they found the King of the Jews in a humble dwelling in Bethlehem.

All this has something to say to us today. We do well to repeat the question asked by the Magi: "Where is the child who has been born the King of the Jews? For we observed his star at its rising, and have come to pay him homage" (Mt 2:2). We are impelled, especially in an age like our own, to seek the signs which God offers us, realizing that great effort is needed to interpret them and thus to understand his will. We are challenged to go to Bethlehem, to find the Child and his Mother. Let us follow the light which God offers us—that tiny light. The hymn in the breviary poetically tells us that the Magi *lumen requirunt lumine*—that tiny light. The light which streams from the face of Christ, full of mercy and fidelity. And once we have found him, let us worship him with all our heart, and present him with our gifts: our freedom, our understanding and our love. True wisdom lies concealed in the face of this Child.

What Stars Do We Follow in Our Lives?

Yet we can also ask why, among all those who looked up at the heavens, so many others did not follow that star, "his star" (Mt 2:2). Perhaps because the star was not eye-catching, did not shine any brighter than other stars. It was a star—so the Gospel tells us—that the Magi saw "at its rising" (vv. 2, 9). Jesus' star does not dazzle or overwhelm, but gently invites. We may ask ourselves what star we have chosen to follow in our lives. Some stars may be bright, but they do not point the way. So it is with success, money, career, honors, and pleasures when these become our life. They are meteors: they blaze momentarily, but then quickly burn out and their brilliance fades. They are shooting stars that mislead rather than lead. The Lord's star, however, may not always overwhelm by its brightness, but it is always there, ever kindly: it takes you by the hand in life and accompanies you. It does not promise material reward, but ensures peace and grants, as it did to the Magi, "exceedingly great joy" (Mt 2:10). But it also tells us to set out.

Let's Look for the Right Light

The Gospel says that they had "seen his star in the East" (Mt 2:2) and they chose to follow it: they chose to be guided by the star of Jesus.

In our life too, there are several stars, lights that twinkle and guide. It is up to us to choose which ones to follow. For example, there are *flashing lights* that come and go, like the small pleasures of life: though they may be good, they are not enough, because they do not last long, and they do not leave the peace we seek. Then there is the *dazzling limelight* of money and success which promises everything, and at once. It is seductive, but with its intensity, blinds and causes dreams of glory to fade into the thickest darkness. The Magi, instead, invite us to follow a *steady light*, a *gentle light* that does not wane, because it is not of this world: it comes from heaven and shines ... where? In the heart.

This true light is the light of the Lord, or rather, *it is the Lord himself*. He is our light: a light that does not dazzle but accompanies and bestows a unique joy. This light is for everyone, and it calls each one of us. In this way, we can hear addressed to us today's invitation from the prophet Isaiah: "Arise, shine" (60:1). So said Isaiah, prophesying this joy of today in Jerusalem, "Arise, shine." At the beginning of each day, we can welcome this invitation: *arise, shine*, and follow today—among the many shooting stars in the world—the bright star of Jesus! Following it, we will experience the joy, as happened to the Magi, who "when they saw the star, they rejoiced exceedingly with great joy" (Mt 2:10); because *where there is God, there is joy*. Those who have encountered Jesus have experienced the miracle of light that pierces the darkness and know this light that illuminates and brightens. I would like, with great respect, to invite everyone not to fear this light and to open up to the Lord. Above all, I would like to say to those who have lost the strength to seek, who are tired, to those who, overwhelmed by the darkness of life, have extinguished this yearning: arise, take heart, the light of Jesus can overcome the deepest darkness. Arise, take heart!

And how do we find this divine light? We follow the example of the Magi, whom the Gospel describes as *always on the move.* He who wants the light, in fact, goes out of himself and seeks: he is not withdrawn, immobile, watching what is happening around him, but rather, he puts his own life at stake; he goes out of himself. Christian life is a *continuous journey*, made of hope, a quest; a journey which, like that of the Magi, continues even when the star momentarily disappears from view. On this journey there are also pitfalls that should be avoided: superficial and mundane gossip, which slows the pace; the paralyzing selfish whims; the pit of pessimism that ensnares hope. These obstacles hindered the scribes, of whom today's Gospel speaks. They knew where the light was, but did not move. When Herod asked them, 'Where will the Messiah be born?' [They answered], 'In Bethlehem!'. They knew where, but did not budge. Their knowledge was vain: they knew many things, but it was useless, all in vain. It is not enough to know that God is born, if you do not celebrate with him *Christmas in the heart.* God is born, yes, but is he born in your heart? Is he born in my heart? Is he born in our hearts? And in this way, we will find him, as did the Magi, with Mary and Joseph in the stable.

We Are Not Abandoned

When the Magi, the Gospel says, "saw the star, they rejoiced exceedingly" (Mt 2:10). For us too, there is great comfort in seeing the star, in other words in feeling guided and not abandoned to our fate. The star is the Gospel, the Word of the Lord, as the Psalm states: "Thy word is a lamp to my feet and a light to my path" (119[118]:105). This light guides us to Christ. Without listening to the Gospel, it is impossible to encounter him! The Wise Men, indeed, by following the star arrived at the place where they found Jesus.

Herod

When Herod realized that he had been outwitted by
the Magi, he was furious, and he gave orders to kill
all the boys in Bethlehem and its vicinity who were
two years old and under, in accordance with the time
he had learned from the Magi.

—Matthew 2:16

(Herod is found in Jerusalem and not in Bethlehem,
but in many Nativity scenes in Spain and Latin America,
Herod's palace is represented and sometimes Herod
himself; also in Italy, in Neapolitan Nativity scenes.)

Herod's Gloomy Palace

The Gospel tells us that the Magi, when they arrived in Jerusalem, lost sight of the star for a time. They no longer saw it. Its light was particularly absent from the palace of King Herod: his dwelling was gloomy, filled with darkness, suspicion, fear, envy. Herod, in fact, proved himself distrustful and preoccupied with the birth of a frail Child whom he thought of as a rival. In reality Jesus came not to overthrow him, a wretched puppet, but to overthrow the Prince of this world! Nonetheless, the king and his counsellors sensed that the foundations of their power were crumbling. They feared that the rules of the game were being turned upside down, that appearances were being unmasked. A whole world built on power, on success, possessions and corruption was being thrown into crisis by a child! Herod went so far as to kill the children. As Saint Quodvultdeus writes, "You destroy those who are tiny in body because fear is destroying your heart" (*Sermo 2 de Symbolo: PL* 40, 655). This was in fact the case: Herod was fearful and on account of this fear, he became insane.

Herod Does Not Know How to Adore

This diligent searching of the Magi contrasts with the second attitude: the *indifference* of the high priests and the scribes. These people are very complacent. They know the Scriptures and are able to give the correct answer on the birthplace: "in Bethlehem of Judea; for so it is written by the prophet" (v. 5); they know, but they do not go out of their way to visit the Messiah. And Bethlehem is a few miles away, but they don't budge.

Even more negative is the third attitude, that of Herod: fear. He *is afraid* that that Child will take away his power. He summons the Magi and has them tell him when the star appeared to them and he sends them to Bethlehem saying: "Go and search diligently for the child and when you have found him, bring me word, that I too may come and worship him" (v. 8). In reality, Herod does not want to go to worship Jesus; Herod wants to know where the child is—not to adore Him—but to eliminate Him, because he considers Him a rival. And listen carefully: fear always leads to hypocrisy. Hypocrites are like this because their hearts are filled with fear....

Selfishness can lead us to consider Jesus' coming into our life as a threat. Thus we try to suppress or to silence Jesus' message. When we follow human ambitions, the most comfortable prospects, tendencies toward evil, Jesus is perceived as an obstacle.

On the other hand, the temptation of indifference is also always present. Even though we know that Jesus is the Savior—ours, of us all—we prefer to live as if he were not: instead of behaving in coherence with our own Christian faith, we follow worldly principles that entice us to satisfy tendencies toward arrogance, toward thirsting for power, toward riches.

Herod Adores Himself

As the Magi made their way, Jerusalem slept. It slept in collusion with a Herod who, rather than seeking, also slept. He slept, anesthetized by a cauterized conscience. He was bewildered, afraid. It is the bewilderment which, when faced with the newness that revolutionizes history, closes in on itself and its own achievements, its knowledge, its successes. The bewilderment of one who sits atop his wealth yet cannot see beyond it. The bewilderment lodged in the hearts of those who want to control everything and everyone. The bewilderment of those immersed in the culture of winning at any cost, in that culture where there is only room for "winners," whatever the price. A bewilderment born of fear and foreboding before anything that challenges us, calls into question our certainties and our truths, our ways of clinging to the world and this life. And so Herod was afraid, and that fear led him to seek security in crime: "You kill the little ones in their bodies, because fear is killing you in your heart" (Saint Quodvultdeus, *Sermon 2 on the Creed:* PL 40, 655). You kill the little ones in their bodies, because fear is killing you in your heart....

Herod is unable to worship because he could not or would not change his own way of looking at things. He did not want to stop worshipping himself, believing that everything revolved around him. He was unable to worship, because his aim was to make others worship him. Nor could the priests worship, because although they had great knowledge, and knew the prophecies, they were not ready to make the journey or to change their ways.

Worship, not Theology, Is Needed: The Meaning of Adoration

In addition to Herod, other people in the Gospel are incapable of worship: they are the chief priests and the scribes. They tell Herod with great precision where the Messiah is to be born: in Bethlehem of Judea (cf. v. 5). They know the prophecies and can quote them exactly. They know where to go—they are great theologians, great!—but they do not go there. Here too we can draw a lesson. In the Christian life, it is not enough to be knowledgeable: unless we step out of ourselves, unless we encounter others and worship, we cannot know God. Theology and pastoral effectiveness mean little or nothing unless we bend the knee; unless we kneel down like the Magi, who were not only knowledgeable about planning a journey, but also capable of setting out and bowing down in worship. Once we worship, we come to realize that faith is not simply a set of fine doctrines, but a relationship with a living Person whom we are called to love. It is in encountering Jesus face to face that we come to see him as he is. Through worship, we discover that the Christian life is a love story with God, where what really matters is not our fine ideas but our ability to make him the center of our lives, as lovers do with those whom they love. This is what the Church ought to be, a worshipper in love with Jesus her spouse....

May we discover anew that faith demands worship. If we can fall on our knees before Jesus, we will overcome the temptation to set off on our own path. For worship involves making an exodus from the greatest form of bondage: slavery to *oneself*. Worship means putting the Lord at the center, not ourselves. It means giving things their rightful place, and giving the first place to God. Worship means making God's plan more important than our personal time, our entitlements and our spaces. It is to accept the teaching of Scripture: "You shall worship the Lord your God" (Mt 4:10). *Your* God: worship means realizing that you and God belong together, to one another. It means being able to speak to him freely and intimately. It means bringing our lives to him and letting him enter into them. It means letting his consolation come down to earth. Worship means discovering that, in order to pray, it is enough to say: "My Lord and my God!" and to let ourselves be pervaded by his tender love.

Christmas Is Also Accompanied by Tears

Christmas is also accompanied, whether we like it or not, by tears. The Evangelists did not disguise reality to make it more credible or attractive. They did not indulge in words that were comforting but unrelated to reality. For them, Christmas was not a flight to fantasy, a way of hiding from the challenges and injustices of their day. On the contrary, they relate the birth of the Son of God as an event fraught with tragedy and grief. Quoting the prophet Jeremiah, Matthew presents it in the bluntest of terms: "A voice is heard in Ramah, wailing and loud lamentation, Rachel weeping for her children" (2:18). It is the sobbing of mothers bewailing the death of their children in the face of Herod's tyranny and unbridled thirst for power.

Today too, we hear this heart-rending cry of pain, which we neither desire nor are able to ignore or to silence. In our world—I write this with a heavy heart—we continue to hear the lamentation of so many mothers, of so many families, for the death of their children, their innocent children.

Herod Drives Away the Holy Family

When Herod's violent rage fell upon the territory of Bethlehem, the Holy Family of Nazareth experienced the anguish of persecution and, guided by God, took refuge in Egypt. Little Jesus reminds us in this way that half of the displaced people in the world today are children, blameless victims of human injustice.

The Holy Family

When Joseph and Mary had done everything required
by the Law of the Lord, they returned to Galilee to
their own town of Nazareth. And the child grew and
became strong; he was filled with wisdom, and the
grace of God was on him.

—Luke 2:39-40

The Son of God Was Born into a Family

It is good to reflect on the fact that the Son of God wanted to
be in need of the warmth of a family, like all children. Precisely
for this reason, because it is Jesus' family, the family of Nazareth
is the model family, in which all families of the world can find
their sure point of reference and sure inspiration. In Nazareth,
the springtime of the human life of the Son of God began to
blossom at the moment he was conceived by the work of the
Holy Spirit in the virginal womb of Mary. Within the welcoming
walls of the House of Nazareth, Jesus' childhood unfolded in
joy, surrounded by the maternal attention of Mary and the care
of Joseph, in whom Jesus was able to see God's tenderness (cf.
Apostolic Letter *Patris Corde*, 2).

In imitation of the Holy Family, we are called to rediscover
the educational value of the family unit: it requires being founded on the love that always regenerates relationships, opening up
horizons of hope. Within the family one can experience sincere
communion when it is a house of prayer, when affections are

serious, profound, pure, when forgiveness prevails over discord, when the daily harshness of life is softened by mutual tenderness and serene adherence to God's will. In this way, the family opens itself up to the joy that God gives to all those who know how to give joyfully. At the same time, it finds the spiritual energy to be open to the outside world, to others, to serving brothers and sisters, to cooperation in building an ever new and better world; capable, therefore, of becoming a bearer of positive stimuli; the family evangelizes by the example of life.

A Family in Remote Places, But Real

The Incarnation of the Son of God opens a new beginning in the universal history of man and woman. And this new beginning happens within a family, in Nazareth. Jesus was born in a family. He could have come in a spectacular way, or as a warrior, an emperor.... No, no: he is born in a family, in a family. This is important: to perceive in the Nativity this beautiful scene.

God chose to come into the world in a human family, which He himself formed. He formed it in a remote village on the outskirts of the Roman Empire. Not in Rome, which was the capital of the Empire, not in a big city, but on its nearly invisible outskirts, indeed, of little renown. The Gospels also recall this, almost as an expression: "Can anything good come out of Nazareth?" (Jn 1:46). Perhaps, in many parts of the world, we still talk this way, when we hear the name of some areas on the periphery of a big city. And so, right there, on the outskirts of the great Empire, began the most holy and good story of Jesus among men! And that is where this family was.

Jesus dwelt on that periphery for thirty years. The Evangelist Luke summarizes this period like this: Jesus "was obedient to them"—that is, to Mary and Joseph. And someone might say: "But did this God, who comes to save us, waste thirty years there, in that suburban slum?" He wasted thirty years! He wanted this. Jesus' path was in that family—"and his mother kept all these things in her heart. And Jesus increased in wisdom and in stature, and in favor with God and man" (Lk 2:51-52). It does not recount miracles, or healing, or preaching—He did none in that period—or of crowds flocking; in Nazareth everything seemed to happen "normally," according to the customs of a pious and hardworking Israelite family: they worked, the mother cooked, she did all the housework, ironed shirts... all the things mothers do. The father, a carpenter, worked, taught his son the trade. Thirty years. "But what a waste, Father!" God works in mysterious ways. But what was important there was the family! And this was not a waste! They were great saints: Mary, the most holy woman, immaculate, and Joseph, a most righteous man.... The family.

Jesus Is the Son of His Family History

God chose a humble and simple family by which to come into our midst. Let us contemplate in amazement the beauty of this mystery, also highlighting two concrete aspects for our families.

The first: *the family is the story from which we originate*. Each of us has our own story. None of us was born magically, with a magic wand. Each of us has our own story and the family is the story from which we originate. The Gospel of today's liturgy reminds us that Jesus too is the son of a family story. We see him travelling to Jerusalem with Mary and Joseph for the Passover; then he makes his Mom and Dad worry when they cannot find him; found again, he returns home with them (cf. Lk 2:41-51). It is beautiful to see Jesus inserted into the fabric of familial affections, which were born and grew in the caresses and concerns of his parents. This is important for us as well: we come from a story that was woven with bonds of love, and the person we are today was born not so much out of the material goods that we enjoyed, but from the love that we received, from the love in the heart of the family. We may not have been born into an exceptional family without problems, but this is our story—everyone must think: this is my story—these are our roots: if we cut them off, life dries up! God did not create us to be lone rangers, but to walk together. Let us thank him and pray to him for our families. God thinks about us and wants us to be together: grateful, united, capable of preserving our roots. And we have to think about this, about our own story.

The second aspect: *we learn how to be a family*, each day. In the Gospel, we see that even in the Holy Family things did not all go well: there were unexpected problems, anxiety, suffering. The Holy Family of holy cards does not exist. Mary and Joseph lose Jesus and search for him anxiously, only to find him three days later. And when, seated among the teachers in the Temple, he responds that he had to be about his Father's business, they do not understand. They need time to learn to know their son. So it is with us too: Every day, families must learn to listen and understand one another, to walk together, to face conflicts and difficulties. It is a daily challenge and it is overcome with the right attitude, through simple actions, simple gestures, caring for the details of our relationships. And this too helps us a lot in order to talk within the family, talk at table, dialogue between parents and children, dialogue among siblings. It helps us experience our family roots that come from our grandparents. Dialogue with the grandparents!

The Family Is a Domestic Church

The nuclear family of Jesus, Mary, and Joseph is for each believer and especially for families an authentic school of the Gospel. Here we admire the fulfilment of the divine plan to make of the family a special community of life and love. Here we learn that every Christian nuclear family is called to be a "domestic church," to make the Gospel virtues shine and become a leaven of good in society. The classic traits of the Holy Family are: reflection and prayer, mutual understanding and respect, and a spirit of sacrifice, work, and solidarity.

From the exemplary witness of the Holy Family, each family can find precious guidance for the style and choices of life, and can draw strength and wisdom for each day's journey. Our Lady and Joseph teach us to welcome children as a gift of God, to beget them and raise them, cooperating wonderfully in the work of the Creator and giving to the world, in each child, a new smile. It is in a united family that children bring their existence to maturity, living out the meaningful and effective experience of freely given love, tenderness, reciprocal respect, mutual understanding, forgiveness, and joy.

I would like to pause above all on joy. The true joy which is experienced in the family is not something random and fortuitous. It is a joy produced by deep harmony among people, which allows them to savor the beauty of being together, of supporting each other on life's journey. However, at the foundation of joy there is always the presence of God, his welcoming, merciful, and patient love for all. If the door of the family is not open to the presence of God and to his love, then the family loses its harmony, individualism prevails, and joy is extinguished. Instead, the family which experiences joy—the joy of life, the joy of faith—communicates it spontaneously, is the salt of the earth, and light of the world, the leaven for all of society.

Parents Are the Guardians of the Children (Not the Owners)

The Gospel invites us to reflect on the experience lived by Mary, Joseph, and Jesus, as they grow together as a family in mutual love and in trust in God. The rite performed by Mary and Joseph, in offering their son Jesus to God, is an expression of this trust. The Gospel states: "they brought him up to Jerusalem to present him to the Lord" (Lk 2:22) as Mosaic Law required. Jesus' parents go to the Temple to attest that their son belongs to God and that they are the guardians of his life, and not the owners. And this leads us to reflect. All parents are guardians of their children's lives, not the owners, and they must help them to grow, to mature.

This gesture emphasizes that God alone is the Lord of individual and family history; everything comes to us from him. Each family is called to acknowledge this primacy, by protecting and educating children to open themselves to God who is the very source of life. From here passes the secret of inner youth, paradoxically witnessed to in the Gospel by an elderly couple, Simeon and Anna. The elderly Simeon, in particular, inspired by the Holy Spirit, says in regard to the Child Jesus: "this child is set for the fall and rising of many in Israel, and for a sign that is spoken against ... that thoughts out of many hearts may be revealed" (vv. 34-35).

There is no family situation that is precluded from this new journey of rebirth and resurrection. Each time that families—even those that are wounded and marked by frailty, failures, and difficulties—return to the source of the Christian experience, new roads and unexpected opportunities open.

Today's Gospel narrative recounts that when Mary and Joseph "had performed everything according to the law of the Lord, they returned into Galilee to their own city, Nazareth. And the child grew"—the Gospel says—"and became strong, filled with wisdom; and the favor of God was upon him" (vv. 39-40). Children's growth is a great joy for the family, we all know it. They are destined to grow and become strong, to acquire knowledge, and receive the grace of God, just as happened to Jesus. He is truly one of us: the Son of God becomes a child, agrees to grow, to become strong; he is filled with knowledge, and the grace of God is upon him. Mary and Joseph have the joy of seeing all this in their son; and this is the mission to which the family is directed: to create conditions favorable to the harmonious and full growth of its children, so they may live a good life, worthy of God and constructive for the world.

Mary, Joseph, and Jesus Help Each Other Discover God's Plan

The term "holy" places this family within the sphere of holiness, which is a gift from God but, at the same time, is free and responsible adherence to God's plan. This was the case for the family of Nazareth: they were totally available to God's will.

How can we not wonder, for example, at Mary's docility to the action of the Holy Spirit Who asks her to become the mother of the Messiah? Because Mary, like every young woman of her time, was about to realize her life project, that is, to marry Joseph.

But when she realizes that God is calling her to a particular mission, she does not hesitate to proclaim herself His "servant" (cf. Lk 1:38). Jesus will exalt her greatness not so much for her role as a mother, but for her obedience to God. Jesus said: "Blessed rather are those who hear the word of God and keep it" (Lk 11:28), like Mary. And when she does not fully understand the events that involve her, Mary meditates in silence, reflects, and adores the divine initiative. Her presence at the foot of the cross consecrates this total willingness.

Then, with regard to Joseph, the Gospel does not give us a single word: he does not speak, but he acts, obeying. He is the man of silence, the man of obedience.

The Gospel reading (Mt 2:13-15, 19-23) recalls this obedience of the righteous Joseph three times, referring to the flight to Egypt and the return to the land of Israel. Under God's guidance, represented by the angel, Joseph distances his family from Herod's threats, and saves them. The Holy Family is thus in solidarity with all the families of the world forced into exile, in solidarity with all those who are compelled to abandon their own land due to repression, violence, and war.

Finally, the third person of the Holy Family, Jesus. He is the will of the Father: in Him, says Saint Paul, there was no "yes" and "no," but only "yes" (cf. 2 Cor 1:19). And this is made manifest in many moments of His earthly life. For example, the episode at the temple when He responded to the anguished parents who sought Him out: "Did you not know that I must be in my Father's house?" (Lk 2:49); His continual repetition: "My food is to do the will of Him Who sent me and to accomplish His work" (Jn 4:34); His prayer in the olive grove: "My Father, if this cannot pass unless I drink it, Your will be done" (Mt 26:42). All these events are the perfect realization of the very words of Christ Who says: "Sacrifices and offerings you have not desired [...] Then I said, 'Behold, I have come to do your will, O God, as it is written of me in the scroll of the book" (Heb 10:5-7; Psalm 40:7-9).

Mary, Joseph, Jesus: the Holy Family of Nazareth which represents a choral response to the will of the Father: the three members of this family help each other reciprocally to discover God's plan. They prayed, worked, communicated. And I ask myself: you, in your family, do you know how to communicate or are you like those kids at the table, each one with their mobile phone, while they are chatting? In that table there seems to be a silence as if they were at Mass... But they do not communicate between themselves. We must resume dialogue in the family: fathers, parents, sons, grandparents, and siblings must communicate with one another ... This is today's homework, on the example of the Holy Family. May the Holy Family be a model for our families, so that parents and children may support each other mutually in adherence to the Gospel, the basis of the holiness of the family.

The Various Statues

The blacksmith, the miller, the water bearer,
the children, the animals…

Many Characters Around Jesus

It is customary to add many symbolic figures to our Nativity scenes. First, there are the beggars and the others who know only the wealth of the heart. They too have every right to draw near to the Infant Jesus; no one can evict them or send them away from a crib so makeshift that the poor seem entirely at home. Indeed, the poor are a privileged part of this mystery; often they are the first to recognize God's presence in our midst.…

Children—but adults too!—often love to add to the Nativity scene other figures that have no apparent connection with the Gospel accounts. Yet, each in its own way, these fanciful additions show that in the new world inaugurated by Jesus there is room for whatever is truly human and for all God's creatures. From the shepherd to the blacksmith, from the baker to the musicians, from the women carrying jugs of water to the children at play: all this speaks of the everyday holiness, the joy of doing ordinary things in an extraordinary way, born whenever Jesus shares his divine life with us.

If We Welcome Him, Everything Can Change

From the Nativity scene we can grasp a teaching on the very meaning of life. We see everyday scenes: shepherds with their sheep, blacksmiths forging iron, millers making bread. Sometimes there are landscapes and circumstances from our areas. It is right because the Nativity scene reminds us that Jesus comes into our concrete lives. And this is important. Always make a small Nativity scene at home because it is a reminder that God came to us; he was born among us, he accompanies us throughout our lives. He is man like we are. He became man like us. In everyday life, we are no longer alone. He abides in us. He does not magically change things but if we welcome Him, everything can change.

The Christmas Tree

The fruit of the righteous is a tree of life.

—Proverbs 11:30

The Tree Points Upwards

Each year the Nativity scene and Christmas tree speak to us through their symbolic language. They render more visible what is understood from the experience of the birth of the Son of God. They are the signs of the heavenly Father's compassion, of his interest in and closeness to humanity, which does not feel abandoned in the darkest of times but sought out and accompanied in its difficulties.

The tree reaching upward spurs us to reach for "the higher gifts" (cf. 1 Cor 12:31), to rise up above the cloudy haze in order to experience how beautiful and joyful it is to be immersed in the light of Christ. In the simplicity of the Nativity, we encounter and contemplate God's tenderness, manifested in that of the Baby Jesus.

A Sign of Rebirth

The tree will remain next to the crib until the end of the Christmas season and will be admired by pilgrims from many places. The fir tree is a sign of Christ, the tree of life (cf. Rev 2:7), a tree to which man had no access because of sin (cf. Gen 2:9). But with Christmas, divine life is joined to human life. The Christmas tree, then, evokes rebirth, the gift of God who unites himself with man forever, who gives us his life. The lights of the fir tree recall that of Jesus, the light of love that continues to shine in the nights of the world.

Dear friends, Christmas is this; let us not let it be polluted by consumerism and indifference. Its symbols, especially the Nativity scene and the decorated tree, bring us back to the certainty that fills our hearts with peace, to the joy of the Incarnation, to God who becomes familiar: he lives with us, he gives a rhythm of hope to our days. The tree and the Nativity scene introduce us to the typical Christmas atmosphere that is part of the heritage of our communities: an atmosphere of tenderness, sharing, and family intimacy. Please, let us not experience a fake Christmas, a commercial Christmas! Let us allow ourselves to be enveloped by the closeness of God, this closeness that is compassionate, that is tender; enveloped by the Christmas atmosphere that art, music, songs and traditions bring to our hearts.

Christmas

For the grace of God has appeared that offers salvation to all people. It teaches us to say 'No' to ungodliness and worldly passions, and to live self-controlled, upright and godly lives in this present age, while we wait for the blessed hope—the appearing of the glory of our great God and Savior, Jesus Christ.

—Titus 2:11-13

The Gift of the Child Jesus

I would like to reflect with you on the Birth of Jesus, the feast of trust and of hope which overcomes uncertainty and pessimism. And the reason for our hope is this: God is with us and God still trusts us! Think well on this: God is with us and God still trusts us. God the Father is generous. He comes to abide with mankind, he chooses earth as his dwelling place to remain with people and to be found where man passes his days in joy or in sorrow. Therefore, earth is no longer only "a valley of tears"; rather, it is the place where God himself has pitched his tent, the meeting place of God with man, of God's solidarity with men.

God willed to share in our human condition to the point of becoming one with us in the Person of Jesus, who is true Man and true God. However, there is something even more surprising. The presence of God among men did not take place in a perfect, idyllic world but rather in this real world, which is marked by so many things both good and bad, by division, wickedness, poverty, arrogance, and war. He chose to live in our history as it is, with all the weight of its limitations and of its tragedies. In doing so, he has demonstrated in an unequalled manner his merciful and truly loving disposition toward the human creature. He is God-with-us. Jesus is God-with-us. Do you believe this? Together let us profess: Jesus is God with us! Jesus is God with us always and forever with us in history's suffering and sorrow. The Birth of Jesus reveals that God "sided" with man once and for all, to save us, to raise us from the dust of our misery, from our difficulty, from our sins.

Hence the great "gift" of the Child of Bethlehem: He brings us a spiritual energy, an energy which helps us not to despair in our struggle, in our hopelessness, in our sadness, for it is an energy that warms and transforms the heart. Indeed, the Birth of Jesus brings us the good news that we are loved immensely and uniquely by God, and he not only enables us to know this love, he also gives it to us, he communicates it to us!

Christmas Is a Perennial Fire

Christmas has become a universal feast, and even those who do not believe perceive the appeal of this occasion. A Christian, however, knows that Christmas is a decisive event, an eternal fire that God has kindled in the world, and must not be confused with ephemeral things. It is important that it not be reduced to a merely sentimental or consumerist festivity.... No: Christmas must not be reduced to a merely sentimental or consumerist feast, full of gifts and good wishes but poor in Christian faith, and also poor in humanity. Therefore, it is necessary to curb a certain worldly mentality, incapable of grasping the incandescent core of our faith, which is this: "And the Word became flesh and dwelt among us, full of grace and truth; we have beheld his glory, glory as of the only Son from the Father" (Jn 1:14). And this is the heart of Christmas; rather, it is the truth of Christmas, there is no other.

Christmas invites us to reflect, on the one hand, on the drama of history, in which men and women, wounded by sin, are unceasingly in search of truth, in search of mercy, and in search of redemption; and, on the other hand, of the goodness of God, who came toward us to communicate to us the Truth that saves and to make us share in his friendship and his life. And this gift of grace: this is *pure* grace, not by any merit of our own…. The Second Vatican Council, in a famous passage from the Constitution on the Church in the Modern World, tells us that this event concerns every one of us: "For by His incarnation the Son of God has united Himself in some fashion with every man. He worked with human hands, He thought with a human mind, acted by human choice, and loved with a human heart. Born of the Virgin Mary, He has truly been made one of us, like us in all things except sin" (Pastoral Constitution *Gaudium et Spes*, 22). But Jesus was born 2,000 years ago, and this pertains to me?—Yes, it pertains to you and me, to each one of us. Jesus is one of us: God, in Jesus, is one of us.

This reality gives us much joy and courage. God did not look down on us from afar, he did not pass us by, he was not repulsed by our misery, he did not clothe himself only superficially in a body, but rather he fully assumed our nature and our human condition. He left nothing out, except sin: the only thing he does not have. All humanity is in him. He took all that we are, just as we are. This is essential for understanding the Christian faith. Saint Augustine, reflecting on his journey of conversion, writes in his *Confessions*: "For I did not hold to my Lord Jesus Christ, I, humbled, to the Humble; nor knew I yet whereto His infirmity would guide us" (*Confessions* VII , 8). And what is Jesus' "infirmity"? The "infirmity" of Jesus is a "teaching"! Because it reveals to us the love of God. Christmas is the feast of Love incarnate, of love born for us in Jesus Christ. Jesus Christ is the light of mankind shining in the darkness, giving meaning to human existence and to the whole of history.

Dear brothers and sisters, may these brief reflections help us to celebrate Christmas with greater awareness. But there is another way to prepare ourselves, which I want to remind you and me, and which is within everyone's reach: to contemplate a little, in silence, before the Nativity scene.... Let us ask for the grace of wonder: before this mystery, a reality so tender, so beautiful, so close to our hearts, that the Lord may give us the grace of wonder, to encounter him, to draw closer to him, to draw closer to us all. This will revive tenderness in us ... the human tenderness close to that of God. And today we are in great need of tenderness, in great need of a human caress, in the face of so much misery!

From Christmas a Certainty: God Is Close to Us

The Liturgy this Sunday sets before us, in the Prologue of the Gospel of St. John, the most profound significance of the Birth of Jesus. He is the Word of God who became man and pitched his "tent," his dwelling, among men. The Evangelist writes: "And the Word became flesh and dwelt among us" (Jn 1:14). These words, that never cease to amaze us, contain the whole of Christianity! God became mortal, fragile like us, he shared in our human condition, except for sin, but he took ours upon himself, as though they were his own. He entered into our history, he became fully God-with-us! The birth of Jesus, then, shows us that God wanted to unite himself to every man and every woman, to every one of us, to communicate to us his life and his joy.

Thus, God is God-with-us, God who loves us, God who walks with us. This is the message of Christmas: the Word became flesh. Thus, Christmas reveals to us the immense love that God has for humanity. From this too derives our enthusiasm, our hope as Christians, that in our poverty we may know that we are loved, that we have been visited, that we are accompanied by God; and we look upon the world and on history as a place in which we walk together with Him and among us toward a new heaven and a new earth. With the Birth of Jesus, a new promise is born, a new world comes into being, but also a world that can be ever renewed. God is always present to stir up new men, to purify the world of the sin that makes it grow old, from the sin that corrupts it. However much human history and the personal story of each of us may be marked by difficulty and weakness, faith in the Incarnation tells us that God is in solidarity with mankind and with human history. This closeness of God to man, to every man and woman, to each one of us, is a gift that never fades! He is with us! He is God-with-us! Behold the glad tidings of Christmas: the divine light that filled the hearts of the Virgin Mary and St. Joseph, and guided the footsteps of the shepherds and the Magi, shines today too for us.

In the Mystery of the Incarnation of the Son of God there is also an aspect that is connected to human freedom, to the freedom of each one of us. Indeed, the Word of God pitched his tent among us, sinners who are in need of mercy. And we all must hasten to receive the grace that he offers us. Instead, the Gospel of St. John continues, "his own people received him not" (v. 11). We reject him too many times, we prefer to remain closed in our errors and the anxiety of our sins. But Jesus does not desist and never ceases to offer himself and his grace which saves us! Jesus is patient. Jesus knows how to wait; he waits for us always. This is a message of hope, a message of salvation, ancient and ever new. And we are called to witness with joy to this message of the Gospel of life, to the Gospel of light, of hope, and of love. For Jesus' message is this: life, light, hope, and love.

Christmas Offers Us Reliable Hope

Isaiah ... foretold the birth of the Messiah in several passages: "Behold, a young woman shall conceive and bear
a son, and shall call his name Immanuel" (7:14); and also:
"there shall come forth a shoot from the stump of Jesse, and
a branch shall grow out of his roots" (11:1). In these passages,
the meaning of Christmas shines through: God fulfills the
promise by becoming man; not abandoning his people, he
draws near to the point of stripping himself of his divinity.
In this way God shows his fidelity and inaugurates a new
Kingdom, which gives *a new hope to mankind*. And what is
this hope? Eternal life.

When we speak of hope, often it refers to what is not in
man's power to realize, which is invisible. In fact, what we
hope for goes beyond our strength and our perception. But
the Birth of Christ, inaugurating redemption, speaks to us
of a different hope, a dependable, visible and understandable
hope, because it is founded in God. He comes into the world
and gives us the strength to walk with him: God walks with
us in Jesus, and walking with him toward the fullness of life
gives us the strength to dwell in the present in a new, albeit
arduous, way. Thus for a Christian, to hope means the certainty of being on a journey with Christ toward the Father who
awaits us. Hope is never still; hope is always journeying, and
it makes us journey. This hope, which the Child of Bethlehem
gives us, offers a destination, a sure, ongoing goal, salvation of
mankind, blessedness to those who trust in a merciful God.
Saint Paul summarizes all this with the expression: "in this
hope we were saved" (Rom 8:24). In other words, walking in
this world, with hope, we are saved. Here we can ask ourselves

the question, each one of us: am I walking with hope or is my interior life static, closed? Is my heart a locked drawer or a drawer open to the hope which enables me to walk—not alone—with Jesus?

Without Jesus There Is No Christmas

In our day, especially in Europe, we are witnessing a type of "distortion" of Christmas: in the name of a false respect which is not Christian, which often hides the wish to marginalize faith, all reference to Christ's birth is eliminated from the holiday. But in reality, this event is the only true Christmas! Without Jesus there is no Christmas; there is another holiday, but not Christmas. And if he is at the center, then all the trimmings, that is, the lights, sounds, various local traditions, including the characteristic foods, all contribute to creating an atmosphere of celebration, but with Jesus at the center. If we remove him, the light goes out and everything becomes feigned, illusory.

Through the message of the Church, we, as the shepherds of the Gospel (cf. Lk 2:9), are led to seek out and find the true light, that of Jesus who, becoming human like us, reveals himself in a surprising way: he is born to a poor, unknown maiden, who gives birth to him in a stable, with only the help of her husband. The world does not notice anything, but in heaven the angels who know of the event exult! And it is in this way that the Son of God presents himself to us today: as God's gift to humanity, which is immersed in darkness and in the listlessness of slumber (cf. Is 9:1). And again today we witness the fact that humanity often prefers darkness, because it knows that the light would reveal all those actions and thoughts that would make us blush or stir our conscience. Thus, we prefer to remain in the dark and not subvert our own bad habits.

We can thus ask ourselves what it means to welcome God's gift, which is Jesus. As he himself has taught us with his life, it means becoming daily a gift freely given to those we meet on our own path. This is why Christmas gifts are exchanged. The true gift to us is Jesus, and like him we seek to be gifts to others. And, since we want to be gifts to others, we exchange gifts, as a sign, as a symbol of this attitude that Jesus teaches us: he, sent by the Father, was a gift to us, and we are gifts to others.

The Apostle Paul offers us a concise key to understanding, when he writes—this passage of Paul is beautiful—"the grace of God has appeared for the salvation of all men, training us ... to live sober, upright, and godly lives in this world" (Tit 2:11-12). The grace of God "has appeared" in Jesus, the face of God, to whom the Virgin Mary gave birth like every child of this world, but he came not "from the earth," he came "from heaven," from God. In this way, with the incarnation of the Son, God opened the way of new life, founded not on selfishness but on love. Jesus' birth is our Heavenly Father's greatest gesture of love.

Dear brothers and sisters, in these days let us open our minds and hearts to welcome this grace. Jesus is God's gift to us and, if we welcome him, we too can become so to others—be a gift of God to others—first and foremost to those who have never experienced attention and tenderness. How many people in our life have never experienced a caress, loving attention, a kind gesture. Christmas spurs us to do so. In this way Jesus comes to be born again in each of our lives and, through us, he continues to be the gift of salvation for the little ones and the excluded.

Christmas Is Celebrating an Unprecedented God

What Christmas would God like, which presents and which surprises?

Let us look at the first Christmas in history to discover God's tastes. That first Christmas in history was *filled with surprises*. It begins with Mary who was betrothed to Joseph. The angel arrives and changes her life. As a virgin, she will become a mother. It continues with Joseph, called to be father to a son without begetting him. A son who—in a dramatic turn of events—arrives at the least appropriate moment, that is, when Mary and Joseph were betrothed and according to the Law, could not live together. Faced with the scandal, the common sense of the time invited Joseph to repudiate Mary and save his good name; but despite this right, he surprises: in order not to shame Mary, he considers leaving her secretly, at the cost of risking his own reputation. Then another surprise: God changes his plans in a dream and asks him to take Mary with him. After Jesus is born and, having plans of his own for his family, once again in a dream, Joseph is told to get up and go to Egypt. Well, Christmas brings unexpected changes to life. And if we want to experience Christmas, we must open our hearts and be ready for surprises, that is, for an unexpected change in life.

But it is on Christmas Eve that the biggest surprise comes: the Almighty is a little Child. The divine Word is an infant, which literally means "unable to speak." And the divine Word became "unable to speak." There are no local authorities of the time nor ambassadors to welcome the Savior: no, there are simple shepherds who, surprised by the angels while they worked at night, hasten without delay. Who would have expected this? Christmas is the celebration of the *'unprecedentedness' of God*, or better, it is the celebration of an *unprecedented God* who overturns our logic and our expectations.

To celebrate Christmas, then, is to receive on earth the surprises of Heaven. We cannot simply live an earthly existence when Heaven has brought its news to the world. Christmas inaugurates a new epoch where life is not planned, but is given: where one no longer lives for oneself, on the basis of one's own taste, but rather for God; and with God because from Christmas onward, God is the God-with-us, who lives with us, who walks with us. To experience Christmas is to allow oneself to be shaken by its surprising newness. The Birth of Jesus does not offer reassuring coziness by the fireside, but rather the divine shudder which shakes history. Christmas is the victory of humility over arrogance, of simplicity over abundance, of silence over clamor, of prayer over "my time," of God over myself.

To *celebrate Christmas* is to do as Jesus did, who came for us needy ones, and to *bend down* to those who need us. It is to do as Mary did: to *trust* God with docility, even without understanding what he will do. To celebrate Christmas is to do as Joseph did: to *arise* in order to do what God wants, even if it is not according to our plans. Saint Joseph is surprising. He never speaks in the Gospel; there is never a word from Joseph in the Gospel, and the Lord speaks to him in silence. He actually speaks to him in his sleep. Christmas means preferring the silent voice of God to the din of consumerism. If we can pause in silence before the Nativity scene, Christmas will be a surprise for us too, not a thing that we have already seen. To stand in silence before the Nativity scene: this is the invitation for Christmas. Take some time, stand before the Nativity scene and be silent. And you will feel, you will understand the surprise.

Unfortunately however, one can have the *wrong celebration* and prefer the usual things of the earth to the newness of Heaven. If Christmas remains just a beautiful traditional celebration where we are at the center and not him, it will be a missed opportunity. Please let us not make Christmas *worldly*! Let us not put the Celebrated One aside, as happened then, when he "came to his own home, and his own people received him not" (Jn 1:11). Ever since the first Gospel of Advent, the Lord has put us on guard, asking us not to weigh ourselves down with "dissipation" and "cares of this life" (Lk 21:34). During these days, we hurry about, perhaps more than at any other time of the year. But in this way, we are doing the opposite of what Jesus wants. We blame the many things that fill the day, the fast-paced world. And yet, Jesus did not blame the world. He asked us not to be dragged in, but to watch at all times, praying (cf. v. 36).

It will be Christmas if, like Joseph, we make room for silence; if like Mary, we say "*here I am*" to God; if, like Jesus, we are close to those who are alone; if, like the shepherds, we leave our enclosure to be with Jesus. It will be Christmas if we find the light in the poor grotto in Bethlehem. *It will not be Christmas* if we seek the glittering brilliance of the world, if we fill ourselves with presents, meals, and dinners but do not help at least one poor person who resembles God because, on Christmas, God came as a poor one.

Dear brothers and sisters, I wish you a Happy Christmas, a Christmas rich in the surprises of Jesus! They may appear to be uncomfortable surprises, but they are God's taste. If we choose them, we will make a splendid surprise for ourselves. Each of us has hidden within the heart the ability to surprise ourselves. Let us allow ourselves to be surprised by Jesus this Christmas.

The Mystery of Christmas Is Humility

If we had to express the entire mystery of Christmas in a word, I believe that *humility* is the one most helpful. The Gospels portray a scene of poverty and austerity, unsuited to sheltering a woman about to give birth. Yet the *King of kings* enters the world not by attracting attention, but by causing a mysterious pull in the hearts of those who feel the thrilling presence of something completely new, something on the verge of changing history. That is why I like to think and also say that *humility was its doorway, and invites us to enter through it....*

It is not easy to understand what humility is. It is the effect of a change that the Spirit himself brings about in us in our daily lives. Such was the case, for example, of Naaman the Syrian (cf. 2 Kings 5). In the days of the prophet Elisha, this man enjoyed great renown. He was a valiant general of the Syrian army who had on many occasions demonstrated his bravery and courage. Yet together with fame, power, esteem, honors and glory, Naaman was forced to live with a tragic situation: he had leprosy. His armor, that had won him renown, in reality covered a frail, wounded, and diseased humanity. We often find this contradiction in our lives: sometimes great gifts are the armor that covers great frailties.

Naaman came to understand a fundamental truth: we cannot spend our lives hiding behind armor, a role we play, or social recognition; in the end, it hurts us. The moment comes in each individual's life when he or she desires to set aside the glitter of this world's glory for the fullness of an authentic life, with no further need for armor or masks. This desire impelled the valiant general Naaman to set out on a journey in search of someone who could help him, and he did this at the suggestion of a slave girl, a Jewish prisoner of war, who told him of a God able to bring healing to hopeless situations like his own.

Laden with silver and gold, Naaman set out on his journey and thus came to the prophet Elisha, who laid down for him, as the only condition for his healing, the simple gesture of disrobing and washing seven times in the Jordan River. Nothing to do with celebrity, honors, gold, or silver! The grace that saves is free; it is not reducible to the price of this world's goods.

Naaman resisted; the prophet's demand seemed to him too ordinary, too simple, too easily attainable. *It seems that the power of simplicity found no room in his imagination.* Yet the words of his servants made him change his mind: "If the prophet had commanded you to do some great thing, would you not have done it? How much rather, then, when he says to you, 'Wash and be clean?'" (2 Kings 5:13). Naaman gave in, and with a gesture of humility "descended," took off his armor, went down into the waters of the Jordan "and his flesh was restored like the flesh of a little child, and he was clean" (2 Kings 5:14). A great lesson, this! The humility of exposing his own humanity, in accordance with the word of the Lord, gained healing for Naaman.

The story of Naaman reminds us that Christmas is a time when each of us needs to find the courage to take off our armor, discard the trappings of our roles, our social recognition and the glitter of this world and adopt the humility of Naaman. We can do this by starting from a more powerful, more convincing and more authoritative example: that of the Son of God who did not shrink from the humility of "descending" into history, becoming man, becoming a child, frail, wrapped in swaddling clothes and laid in a manger (cf. Lk 2:16). Once we strip ourselves of our robes, our prerogatives, positions and titles, all of us are lepers, all of us are in need of healing. Christmas is the living reminder of this realization, and it helps us to understand it more deeply.

A Feeling of Amazement

In these days the liturgy invites us to reawaken in ourselves wonder, wonder at the mystery of the Incarnation. The feast of Christmas is perhaps the one that most arouses this inner attitude: awe, wonder, contemplation.... Like the shepherds of Bethlehem, who first receive the luminous angelic announcement and then rush in and actually find the sign that had been shown to them, the Child wrapped in swaddling clothes in a manger. With tears in their eyes, they kneel before the newborn Savior. But not only they; Mary and Joseph are also filled with holy wonder at what the shepherds report hearing from the angel about the Child.

Just so: Christmas cannot be celebrated without amazement. But an amazement that is not limited to a superficial emotion—this is not amazement—an emotion linked to the externality of the holiday, or even worse, to a consumerist frenzy. No. If Christmas is reduced to this, nothing changes: tomorrow will be the same as yesterday, next year will be the same as last year, and so on. It would mean warming ourselves for a few moments at a straw fire, and not instead exposing ourselves with our whole being to the power of the Event, not grasping the center of the mystery of Christ's birth.

And the center is this: "The Word became flesh and lived among us" (Jn 1:14). We hear it repeatedly in this evening liturgy, with which the solemnity of Mary Most Holy Mother of God opens. She is the first witness, the first and greatest, and at the same time the most humble. The greatest because the most humble. Her heart is filled with amazement, but without a shadow of romanticism, of sentimentality, of spiritualism. No. The Mother takes us back to reality, to the truth of Christmas, which is contained in those four words of Saint Paul: "born of a woman" (Gal 4:4). Christian amazement does not originate from special effects, from fantastic worlds, but from the mystery of reality: there is nothing more wonderful and sentimental than reality! A flower, a clod of earth, a life story, an encounter.… The wrinkled face of an old man and the newly blossomed face of a child. A mother holding her baby in her arms and feeding him at her breast. There, the mystery shines through.

Brothers and sisters, Mary's amazement, the Church's amazement is full of *gratitude.* The gratitude of the Mother who, contemplating her Son, feels God's closeness, feels that God has not abandoned his people, that God has come, that God is near, is God-with-us. Problems have not disappeared, difficulties and worries are not lacking, but we are not alone: the Father "sent his Son" (Gal 4:4) to redeem us from the bondage of sin and restore our dignity as sons and daughters. He, the Only Begotten, became the firstborn among many brothers and sisters to lead all of us, lost and scattered, back to the Father's house.

This time of pandemic has increased the sense of loss throughout the world. After an initial phase of reaction, in which we felt joined in the same boat, the temptation of "everyone for themselves" spread. But thank God we reacted again, with a sense of responsibility. Truly we can and must say "thanks be to God," because the choice of joint responsibility does not come from the world: it comes from God; indeed, it comes from Jesus Christ, who once and for all imprinted in our history the "course" of his original vocation: to be all sisters and brothers, children of the one Father.

Epilogue

Let us pause before the manger to contemplate how God has been present throughout this year and to remind ourselves that every age, every moment is the bearer of graces and blessings. The manger challenges us not to give up on anything or anyone. To look upon the manger means to find the strength to take our place in history without complaining or being resentful, without closing in on ourselves or seeking a means of escape, looking for shortcuts in our own interest. Looking at the manger means recognizing that the times ahead call for bold and hope-filled initiatives, as well as the renunciation of vain self-promotion and endless concern with appearances.

Looking at the manger means seeing how God gets involved by involving us, making us part of his work, inviting us to welcome the future courageously and decisively.

Looking at the manger, we see Joseph and Mary, their young faces full of hopes and aspirations, full of questions. Young faces that look to the future conscious of the difficult task of helping the God-Child to grow. We cannot speak of the future without reflecting on these young faces and accepting the responsibility we have for our young; more than a responsibility, the right word would be debt, yes, the debt we owe them. To speak of a year's end is to feel the need to reflect on how concerned we are about the place of young people in our society.

We are asked to be something other than the innkeeper in Bethlehem who told the young couple: there is no room here. There was no room for life, there was no room for the future. Each of us is asked to take some responsibility, however small, for helping our young people to find, here in their land, in their own country, real possibilities for building a future.

Sources

The Nativity Scene

Christmas greeting to the employees of the Holy See and of Vatican City State, 21 December 2018.

Apostolic Letter *Admirabile Signum* on the Meaning and Importance of the Nativity Scene, 1 December 2019.

General Audience, 18 December 2019.

The Child Jesus

Apostolic Letter *Admirabile Signum* on the Meaning and Importance of the Nativity Scene, 1 December 2019.

General Audience, 1 December 2019.

Homily, 24 December 2021.

Address to the Young People of Italian Catholic Action, 20 December 2013.

"Urbi et Orbi" message, 25 December 2020.

Homily, 24 December 2020.

Angelus, 2 January 2022.

Angelus, 3 January 2021.

General Audience, 18 December 2013.

Address, 21 December 2019.

General Audience, 18 December 2019.

Homily, 24 December 2014.

General Audience, 30 December 2015.

"Urbi et Orbi" message, 25 December 2017.

Homily, 25 May 2014.

Homily, 24 December 2019.

Mary

Homily, 24 December 2017.

Homily, 1 January 2020.

Angelus, 1 January 2022.

Angelus, 20 December 2020.

Angelus, 21 December 2014.

Angelus, 18 December 2016.

Homily, 1 January 2022.

Angelus, 19 December 2021.

Joseph

Angelus, 22 December 2013.

Angelus, 18 December 2022.

Apostolic Letter *Admirabile Signum* on the Meaning and Importance of the Nativity Scene, 1 December 2019.

General Audience, 19 March 2014.

Apostolic Letter *Patris Corde*, 8 December 2020.

Bethlehem

Homily, 24 December 2018.

General Audience, 21 December 2016.

Homily, 24 December 2017.

Homily, 24 December 2021.

The Stable

Apostolic Letter *Admirabile Signum* on the Meaning and
Importance of the Nativity Scene, 1 December 2019.

Homily, 24 December 2018.

Angelus, 22 December 2013.

Homily, 24 December 2016.

The Angels

General Audience, 21 December 2016.

Greetings to the Artists of the Christmas Concert
in the Vatican, 15 December 2021.

The Shepherds

"Urbi et Orbi" message, 25 December 2017.

Homily, 24 December 2017.

Apostolic Letter *Admirabile Signum* on the Meaning and
Importance of the Nativity Scene, 1 December 2019.

Homily, 24 December 2018.

Angelus, 6 January 2016.

Homily, 24 December 2016.

Homily, 24 December 2019.

The Light

Homily, 24 December 2014.

Homily, 24 December 2015.

Homily, 24 December 2019.

Angelus, 6 January 2021.

Angelus, 4 January 2015.

The Magi

Homily, 6 January 2015.

Homily, 6 January 2017.

Homily, 6 January 2022.

Angelus, 6 January 2019.

Apostolic Letter *Admirabile Signum* on the Meaning and
    Importance of the Nativity Scene, 1 December 2019.

Homily, 6 January 2018.

Homily, 6 January 2020.

Angelus, 6 January 2022.

Homily, 6 January 2020.

The Star

Homily, 6 January 2016.

Homily, 6 January 2018.

Angelus, 6 January 2017.

Angelus, 6 January 2016.

Angelus, 27 December 2020.

General Audience, 17 December 2014.

Angelus, 26 December 2021.

Angelus, 27 December 2015.

Angelus, 31 December 2017.

Angelus, 29 December 2019.

Apostolic Letter *Admirabile Signum* on the Meaning and
    Importance of the Nativity Scene, 1 December 2019.

Herod

Homily, 6 January 2014.

Angelus, 6 January 2018.

Homily, 6 January 2017.

Homily, 6 January 2020.

Letter to Bishops on the Feast of the Holy
Innocents, 28 December 2018.

Address to Performers and Organizers of the
Christmas Concert, 14 December 2018.

The Holy Family

Angelus, 27 December 2020.

General Audience, 17 December 2014.

Angelus, 26 December 2021.

Angelus, 27 December 2015.

Angelus, 31 December 2017.

Angelus, 29 December 2019.

The Various Statues

Apostolic Letter *Admirabile Signum* on the Meaning and
Importance of the Nativity Scene, 1 December 2019.

General Audience, 18 December 2019.

The Christmas Tree

Greeting to the Polish and Italian delegations who donated
this year's Christmas Tree and Nativity Scene in
Saint Peter's Square, 7 December 2017.

Address to the delegations which donated the Christmas Tree and Nativity Scene in Saint Peter's Square and in the Paul VI's Hall, 10 December 2021.

Christmas

General Audience, 18 December 2013.

General Audience, 23 December 2020.

Angelus, 5 January 2014.

General Audience, 21 December 2016.

General Audience, 27 December 2017.

General Audience, 19 December 2018.

Address to the Roman Curia, 23 December 2021.

Homily, 31 December 2021.

Epilogue

Homily, 31 December 2016.

FOCOLARE MEDIA

Enkindling the Spirit of Unity

The New City Press book you are holding in your hands is one of the many resources produced by Focolare Media, which is a ministry of the Focolare Movement in North America. The Focolare is a worldwide community of people who feel called to bring about the realization of Jesus' prayer: "That all may be one" (see John 17:21).

Focolare Media wants to be your primary resource for connecting with people, ideas, and practices that build unity. Our mission is to provide content that empowers people to grow spiritually, improve relationships, engage in dialogue, and foster collaboration within the Church and throughout society.

 Visit www.focolaremedia.com to learn more about all of New City Press's books, our award-winning magazine *Living City*, videos, podcasts, events, and free resources.

NEW CITY PRESS